Presented to

_____

By

_____

On the Occasion of

_____

Date

_____

Love Stories
of the BIBLE

Love Stories
of the BIBLE

DARLENE MINDRUP

BARBOUR
PUBLISHING

Published by Barbour Publishing, Inc., P.O. Box 719, Uhrichsville, Ohio 44683 www.barbourbooks.com

Our mission is to publish and distribute inspirational products offering exceptional value and biblical encouragement to the masses.

 Member of the
Evangelical Christian
Publishers Association

Printed in the United States of America.
5 4 3 2 1

CONTENTS

A NOTE FROM THE AUTHOR

The word *Bible* simply translated means "book," and truly it is the greatest book ever written. It took nearly forty authors approximately 1,600 years to write. Its pages are full of stories of treachery, devotion, history, and even love. Yet many of the stories within give us very little information on the times, nor does it share its stories in their entirety.

Using various resources like the Works of Josephus, Jewish tradition, historical and geographical documents, and most importantly, the Bible itself, I have tried to put together stories that are plausible and that give the reader the essence of the time periods involved.

While the stories you are about to read contain fiction, I believe they are true to the integrity of the Bible. I have not tried to add to the Word, but rather, it is my hope, to bring it more fully alive.

In Christ,
Darlene Mindrup

ADAM AND EVE
GENESIS 1:26–3:6

Adam walked by the side of the woman God had presented him with earlier that day. He felt irresistibly drawn to her, wanting nothing more than to look at and touch her.

He marveled at the sameness, yet the differences between them. Whereas he was lean and firmly built, she was soft and full of gentle curves. Her hair hung long to her waist in a black shimmering mass. His had yet to touch his shoulders. His voice was as deep as the river that ran through the garden, yet hers was light, like the butterfly that flitted from plant to plant.

She glanced his way, and their eyes met and held. Did she feel the wonder, too? He had first awakened to a world of light and color with no past memory of any time before. It had never occurred to him that the Creator of the universe had done something so marvelous, so wonderful that it couldn't even have been imagined. Until now. Eve was proof.

He could still feel the tender place on his side where the Lord had used a part of him to fashion this exquisite creature. The wonder was almost too much to bear.

He glanced around the garden realizing for the first time just how phenomenal this creation was. He saw it with new eyes. What must it look like to Eve? What must *he* look like to her?

Reaching out, he took her by the hand. She jerked in surprise, her eyes full of tightly controlled questions. Probably the very same ones that had run through his mind when he had first opened his eyes. Only God had been there for him, just as he was now here for Eve.

"Come this way. I want to show you something."

She allowed her hand to rest in his, and he felt again the thrill of its softness. He took her to where a male lion and its mate lay resting in the warm afternoon sun.

"These are called lions," he told Eve. "The largest is a male, like me. The other is a female, like you."

Soft color bloomed in her cheeks. She didn't look at him, instead going to where the lions lay, and kneeling before them, she ran her fingers through the male's tawny mane. The lion rumbled low in its throat, expressing its pleasure.

As she continued to stroke him, she smiled up at Adam. "He's so soft."

Adam returned her smile. Yes, the lion was indeed soft, but nothing like this beautiful Eve. She belonged to him, yet not really. God had given her to him, but there was a reserve about her that was hard to penetrate. He wondered what she was thinking, but for some reason he was reluctant to ask. In the end, he didn't need to.

She turned to him, her voice full of doubt. "Is this real, Adam? Is all this real?"

He understood what she meant. He, too, had no thoughts that did not constitute the last several hours. When he had awakened, everything that he could see now had already been in existence, yet he could remember nothing of its having come into being. At least the Creator had explained it all to him, but Eve had not spent as much time with Him as Adam had. All he knew was that from the moment the Creator had presented him with this beautiful woman, the emptiness he had felt when witnessing all of the other animals with their mates had disappeared.

He pulled Eve to her feet and did what he had longed to do from the moment he had first set eyes on her. He wrapped her in his arms and held her near. His hands glided over the soft texture of her back, holding her close.

"Eve," he whispered, understanding her confusion. "I am real."

Hesitantly, her hands drifted up his back and settled near his shoulders. He closed his eyes against the sensations that burst through him. Her face nestled against his chest, and he wondered if she could feel his heart drumming against her cheek. Some instinct made him press his lips against the top of her head. She lifted her face to frown up at him.

"I don't understand any of this."

His look rested on the soft fullness of her lips, red like the pomegranate.

"God explained it to me this way," he said softly. "I was created by Him, for Him. You were created by Him, for me."

He could understand her confusion. His own mind was full of the same. Although God had given him the ability to speak and reason, there was just too much that he didn't understand.

"Look around you at the animals that God created," he told her. "Each of them has a purpose."

She studied the animals for a few minutes and then looked up at him. "What is ours?"

He pulled back from her, reluctantly releasing her from his hold. "Ours is to care for the garden."

She nodded, but the confusion never left her face.

"Come. Let me show you," he enjoined her.

It was a thrill to show her the marvels of the garden. At every creature, Eve would squeal with delight. At every plant, the wonder in her eyes grew.

The day passed, and the shadows lengthened. Eve noticed the change and frowned.

"Adam, the light grows dim."

The fear in her eyes pierced his heart. Adam

smiled reassuringly. "The Lord told me that this would be so. The bright light of the sun will cease, and a lesser light of the moon will take its place. It will be a time for us to rest."

He could tell that his words had not convinced her. Having not experienced this night himself, he had to place his faith in the Lord. She would have to do the same.

"Let us find a place to sleep," he told her, and led her to a small glade. He fashioned a resting place under a tree and lay down, motioning for her to join him. It said something for her developing trust in him that she immediately complied.

They lay together watching the sunlight grow ever dimmer and the moon rise to take its place. They both stared in awe as tiny specks of light multiplied in the dark sky until it seemed as though the whole expanse was alive with them.

"Oh, Adam," Eve breathed softly. "It's so beautiful."

Indeed it was, though Adam felt he much preferred the daylight. He pulled Eve closer and she settled her head against his chest. The darkness was a little frightening, but Adam wasn't certain why this was so. He sensed something not quite right in this wonderful paradise, but he could not put a name to it. Something seemed to be waiting just beyond in the darkness, something that didn't belong. His eyes narrowed and he pulled Eve a little closer, his heart rate accelerating, tension coiling his body.

Eve's breathing became soft and steady and Adam knew that she had fallen asleep. It was much later before his own eyes finally fluttered and then closed altogether.

～～～

Eve loved holding and cuddling the baby animals. They were so adorable. Their antics often brought laughter to both Adam and herself.

Although she loved to play with the baby lion cubs, she loved even more nestling close the baby rabbits. They snuggled against her, making her feel warm inside. She wondered how long it would be until it was her turn to bear young. The Lord had said to be fruitful and multiply, and many of the animals had already produced young after their own kind. Each one filled her with awe, and impatience for it to be her turn.

God was so wise, so all-knowing. What must it be like to know everything? Her time on this earth had been so limited compared to God's existence. He had always been. He had told them so. The thought made her mind swim, her head ache. It was beyond her comprehension.

One thing she had noted about the animals, at least the majority of them, was that after mating, the male often left the female. The thought of Adam doing the same left her feeling frightened.

Oh, she knew that if that happened, God would take care of her, just as He did the other animals, but the thought of being left alone with nothing but a child terrified her.

She had finally gotten up the courage to speak with God about it. He had assured her that He had made humans different. He had pointed out to her the animals that had mated and were still a family. Yet they were so few, it hardly reassured her. How could she know for sure?

She had finally mentioned her fears to Adam, and he had taken her into his arms and held her close. He had assured her with words, but he had also tried to assure her with his kisses filled with love. She loved him so much that it hurt inside.

As more and more animals had young and left their mates, the fear grew in her mind that Adam would do the same. He tried to reason with her, but how could he know for certain? He wasn't God. If only she could know for sure. If only she were like God.

❧ ⁓ ❧

Adam walked with Eve through the garden, his delight in his world somewhat tempered by his concern over Eve's preoccupation lately.

He took her hand, once again trying to express through touch the feelings that ran so deep within him. How was it possible to love someone so much? She filled his every waking thought, and many of his sleeping ones, as well.

Lately she had been concerned over whether he would leave her when she bore young. The thought had never even entered his head, but he could understand her concern. They witnessed it every day among the animals.

Still, God had assured them both that humans were created different, created in His own image. Not being God, he didn't fully understand what that meant, but he trusted the Lord.

He could never leave her. The idea didn't even bear thinking about. He would only be half a person without her. She completed him in ways he couldn't explain.

So occupied had been his thoughts, he didn't realize when Eve had left his side. Not until she called his name did he sense that something was amiss.

He turned to her, noting the serpent at her side. Frowning, he approached them both warily.

Eve held out a piece of fruit to him, and he recognized it from the forbidden tree. A bite from the fruit showed that Eve had already sampled it. His eyes went wide, his heart pounding in fear.

"What have you done?" he breathed.

"See, Adam. The Lord was wrong. I did not die." She motioned with the fruit. "Try some. It's really delicious."

That sense of something wrong filled him once again, yet still he could not put a name to it. His narrow-eyed gaze focused on the serpent standing innocently by Eve's side.

The Lord had told him that if he ever ate from the tree, he would be banished from the garden. His heart began to pound with dread. He knew with certainty that the Lord would find out that Eve had gone against His command. She would be sent from the garden, and he would be alone once again.

Yet she hadn't died. Could it be that the Lord was wrong? Could it be that He had not told them the truth? Was there another reason He didn't want them to eat from the tree? Perhaps He was afraid that they would become as wise as He.

If God was wrong about her dying, perhaps He was wrong about other things, as well. Whatever the reason, he couldn't take a chance on being separated from Eve.

The thought of losing her sent pain lancing through his heart. The very thing she was afraid of happening would occur. She would be alone, and so would he. What was paradise without the woman he loved? Before she had come into his life, he had been empty. Even with God there to keep him company, it hadn't been enough.

No, he couldn't take the chance on being separated from Eve. If she was to be punished, then so must he.

He reached for the fruit.

ABRAM AND SARAI
GENESIS 11:27–12:20

Sarai knew she was beautiful. How could she help it? Every day it seemed some man, young or old, would seek her out on one pretext or another. Her father had received so many proposals of marriage it was a wonder that there was any male left in Ur that still hadn't asked for her.

Even now, there were men in the crowd more interested in her than in the sacrifice being offered to Sin, the moon god. Sarai felt nothing but irritation. What good was beauty if it couldn't get you the one thing you wanted most in the world? Why was it that the one man she wanted to notice her as a woman saw her as nothing but a child?

She could see him now, standing across the crowd, frowning at the young men holding the sacred black bull as the high priestess draped a garland around its neck. His short beard reflected the sunlight and glowed a dark amber. His strong, lithe body was held tensely erect.

Abram. Her half brother.

From as far back as she could remember, she had adored him. His infinite patience with her when she was but a child and he was already reaching manhood had won her heart. But he still saw her as nothing more than his little sister.

Father said it was imperative that she marry

within the clan so that their wealth would stay among the family. It was the way of things. The only problem was, Father hoped that she would marry Nahor, and she was firmly set on his older brother.

The golden bracelets on her wrists and ankles jangled as she moved through the crushing throng toward him. The high priestess's words faded into the background when Sarai reached Abram's side and smiled into his serious face.

"Such a face," she scolded softly. She laid a small hand against the dark skin of his forearm and felt him trembling. She glanced up at him in surprise but noted that his mind was certainly not on her. Even with her touch, he was unaware of her presence. She tugged gently at the sleeve of his tunic.

He glanced down, noticing her for the first time, and his face blossomed into an instant smile. Sarai felt some of her ire at his being oblivious to her presence dwindle and then disappear altogether when he spoke.

"If it isn't the most beautiful girl in the world."

Sarai cocked her head slightly, her eyes fueled with intent. The words pleased her; the reference to age did not.

"Woman," she corrected.

She almost laughed at the look of astonishment

on his face. She leaned close until she knew the fragrance of her perfume would reach him, its sultry fragrance evocative enough, she hoped, to generate some response from him.

"Why are you frowning so, Abram? One would think that you objected to the sacrifice."

A strange look passed over his features. She recognized the set of his face that followed and knew that whatever was bothering him, he was not about to share it with her. He glanced down at her and his eyes softened.

"Sarai." He reached out and gently touched his fingers to her jaw, smiling slightly. "Princess. The name fits you, you know."

Sarai felt a little thrill run through her. The look in his eyes started her heart thrumming with the speed of a racing dust storm. Was it possible that Abram was finally beginning to see her as a woman?

"Someday," he went on, "you will probably marry a king."

Now it was her turn to frown. "What foolishness!"

"There isn't a man that I know who doesn't want you," he told her. "Even the king has been casting his eyes your way. Which is why I am here. Father wants you to come home and get ready to move camp."

"Already? But Father never moves camp this

early in the year. I wanted to stay for the rest of the ceremony and the procession."

He glanced over her shoulder and Sarai followed his look. The priestess continued with her invocations, but her eyes were fixed on Sarai. Sarai shuddered at the animosity that gleamed from them. Surprised, she turned back to Abram for an explanation, but he took her by the arm and began leading her away. His continued silence unnerved her.

It took them some time to reach their camp, since it was located several miles from the city. Sarai was hot and tired by the time they returned, not to mention aggravated. She had been anxious to see the barge that would bring Sin into Ur. She had never been a part of the god's ceremonies before, usually being too far away to come, but today she had made the decision to finally see the great moon god.

Nahor met her at the entrance to their family tent.

"Where have you been?" he demanded, and Sarai bristled.

"You are not my husband, Nahor. You have no right to demand explanations from me."

His eyes blackened with his anger. "You know Father wishes us to marry."

Abram passed them, his look a mixture of anger and resignation. Sarai's frustrations mounted. For some time their father had planned a marriage between Abram and Terah's niece. That left Nahor for Sarai. The only one who seemed pleased by the arrangement was Nahor, and though he was about to continue his tirade, Terah called for him from outside the tent. He continued glaring at Sarai for several seconds, then pushed his way past her, his look telling her more clearly than anything that the conversation was far from over.

Her eyes met Abram's and she noticed his look of irritation. For some reason, it made her feel guilty.

"What have I done?" she demanded.

He shook his head slightly. "You have absolutely no idea what your beauty does to a man, do you?"

She should have been pleased; instead she felt the guilt increase.

"I cannot help the way that I look, Abram," she told him softly. In truth, she had often felt her looks to be a curse by the gods.

Abram sighed. "No, that is true." He smiled wryly. "But it has often been a problem for the whole family."

"In what way?" she asked, feeling suddenly cold all over.

"It is the reason we are moving today, during the festival. The king has noticed you, and Father wishes to remove you from his presence before he can take an even greater interest in you. Surely you noticed the priestess's reaction to you today. She is afraid that you will win her father's heart and she will lose her influence with him."

Sarai stared at him open mouthed. "Is this true?"

His sigh was protracted, and coming to her, he took her by the shoulders. "Sarai, Sarai. You are far too innocent." His mouth tilted slightly. "This is not the first time."

Sarai was appalled. She really didn't know what to say. Abram rubbed his hands up and down her arms.

"Never mind. Just go and help get the camp ready to leave."

She took his hand before he could walk away. He turned to her, lifting one eyebrow in question.

"And you, Abram? What do you feel about me?"

Sarai held her breath. She couldn't believe she had been so bold as to ask the question, but it hung in the air between them, demanding an answer. Abram's eyes darkened, his gaze settling on her lips for a brief instant.

"Don't ask me that, Sarai."

He pulled from her hold and walked away, and she felt a heaviness of heart that she had never experienced before.

❧ — ❧

Abram walked away from the tent, his emotions

roiling. Nahor glanced at him suspiciously, but Abram ignored him and went to begin packing their belongings on the donkeys.

He took a deep breath, trying to gain control of himself. He wasn't exactly sure what to do about this growing awareness between Sarai and himself. He recognized her flirtatiousness for what it was and was flattered, but it certainly complicated things.

When had he begun to see Sarai as more than a little sister? How had it happened? Perhaps when Nahor had started showing marked attention to her and proposed his idea of marriage. Until then, he had never really taken a good look at her. She had always been the little girl who followed him around with adoring eyes.

The eyes hadn't changed, but the body certainly had. Her hair hung lustrous and thick down her back, her body that of a nubile young woman. The dark brown of her eyes sent him messages he hadn't heretofore noticed. He would never be able to see her as a child again. Those days were gone forever. So, where did that leave them?

Father had made clear that he wished Abram to marry his uncle's daughter, thus ensuring the two family's wealth would remain intact. Abram had nothing against his cousin, but she was certainly not Sarai.

Then Nahor's rash declaration that he would

kill anyone who tried to take Sarai away from him was unsettling. Still, it wouldn't be the first time someone's life had been threatened because of Sarai, and he sincerely doubted it would be the last. Sarai had no idea what she did to a man. He hoped she never found out.

Although they had many tents, sheep, goats, and donkeys to move, not to mention people, they managed to be on their way by early afternoon.

As they traveled along, Sarai met his look from time to time, and his heart constricted at the pain he saw in her eyes. It had honestly never occurred to him that her affections had been so set on him, and although it shouldn't have, the thought pleased him mightily.

Each day they traveled took them farther from the city of Ur, though its impressive ziggurat to Sin could still be seen in the distance, the temple to a stone god that Abram wasn't certain he still believed in.

Perhaps his questioning had to do with the dreams. Several times he had a dream about a man coming to him, a man who glowed like fire. The light was so intense that Abram could never see the face, but the voice was distinct and clear. The voice that told him there was only one God.

At first he had scoffed, but the more he thought about it, the more likely it seemed that it could be true. After all, a god should be someone who is all-powerful, all-present. He shouldn't be relegated to a house and moved by barge to and fro.

He hadn't yet told his family of the dream, knowing that they would surely laugh at such an idea.

But that nighttime imagery was as nothing compared to the other.

In his dream, he was dressed as a priest and preparing to sacrifice an offering. The offering was a young boy who stared up at him with trusting eyes. Even now, his blood ran cold at the thought. In the dream, as he was about to plunge the knife into the child, he would wake up sweating, his body shaking with stark terror.

He knew about countries where sacrificing people to their gods was an acceptable practice, but he sincerely hoped that the dream wasn't some precursor of his own life. Would he really fall into such a temptation? He didn't like to think it was possible, but wasn't that what dreams were all about?

"What gloomy thoughts are causing your mouth to turn down, my brother?"

Abram hadn't even realized that his younger brother Haran had joined him. He tried to shake off his somber mood. He gave his brother a brief smile.

"Nothing that need concern you," he told him, another smile taking any sting from the words.

Haran studied him a moment but then nodded. "Father says that we will stop near the green spring and stay there for a while."

Abram nodded in return and prepared to make camp.

❧——❧

Father and Uncle Tahor had been in conference with each other for some time. When Uncle Tahor left, Terah followed him from the tent, his face set in angry lines. He motioned Abram inside the tent and told him to take a seat.

Abram folded his legs, sitting on the pillows provided. He was anxious to know what had just transpired between his uncle and his father, for he knew that it had to do with him.

After seating himself among the cushions on the floor and straightening his robes around him, Terah came right to the point. "Your uncle has decided to marry his daughter to a man from Mittani."

Though Abram was surprised, he certainly wasn't dissatisfied. Still, he could tell how angry his father was. His long beard seemed to bristle with his wrath.

"Tahor wishes to join his wealth with a family who has even more wealth."

Abram said nothing. Finally, his father turned to him.

"I had always thought to marry Sarai to Nahor,

but the eldest should marry first. Therefore, I wish for you to marry Sarai."

Abram felt his heart begin to pound, his palms growing sweaty. Only last night when he had had the dream again, he had told the vision, "If You are the only God, give me Sarai to prove it."

Perhaps he hadn't truly believed that the vision was a god, or he would certainly never have dared to make such a request. He wasn't certain what was causing the blood to run so swiftly through his veins now: the thought of the answered prayer or the thought of actually having Sarai for his wife.

"Nahor will not be pleased," Abram reminded his father.

His father's eyes gleamed. "Nahor will do as he is told."

Abram had no doubt that was true. If there was one thing Nahor wanted more than Sarai, it was wealth and land. To incur his father's wrath would cut him off from everything he hoped to gain.

Terah sent a servant to fetch Nahor. When apprised of the events of the afternoon, Nahor lashed out at his father in anger. The older man was unimpressed. He allowed Nahor his say, but in the end, Nahor knew he had no choice. He flung himself from the tent without once looking Abram's way.

Terah's irritation was unassuaged. He glared at

Abram. "Let us put an end to these disputes over Sarai. The marriage will take place in four days."

⌒⌒

Sarai looked out over the plains of Haran and thought over the last forty-eight years. She could still remember the thrill she had felt at becoming Abram's wife. Now he was seventy-five, and she was sixty-five, but her love for him was undiminished. Even now, just the thought of his touch made her feel warm all over.

He had always been so gentle with her. So loving.

That gentleness had extended to his brother, Nahor, as well. For some time after the marriage, Sarai had truly feared for Abram's life. But now Nahor had Milcah, his niece, as his wife. She was so very young compared to Nahor, but he had been kind to her after Haran had died, taking the girl into his home.

Now, they had left Ur behind and were dwelling in the land of Haran. Nahor had refused to come with them, but Haran's grandson Lot had decided that he wanted to.

Terah had at first decided to go to Canaan, but after reaching Haran, he had determined to stay. Perhaps because the name brought back memories of his son. Whatever the reason, here they abided.

The one thing that Sarai regretted the most

was that she had never been able to give Abram a child. She had offered a sacrifice to every god she could remember, but to no avail.

When strong arms wrapped around her middle, she jumped. Turning her head, she encountered Abram's smiling face just inches from her own.

"Do you know that you are as beautiful as the day we married?"

She snuggled into his embrace, turning her gaze back upon the fertile land before her. She rested her crossed arms atop Abram's and smiled.

"If you say so."

He nuzzled his bearded chin against her neck, finding her ticklish spot. She giggled but didn't move away.

Abram released his hold and, taking her by the shoulder, turned her to face him. Suddenly, his face was very serious.

"God talked to me again last night."

Sarai froze. Abram had shared with her his dreams, and though they had diminished over the years, lately they had had a resurgence. The thought of one all-powerful God was more than she could comprehend. She knew of no people near or far that believed such a thing.

"What—what did He say?"

"He said, 'Leave your country, your people, and your father's household and go to the land I will show you.'"

Sarai's lips parted in surprise and she studied her husband's face, trying to fathom his thoughts. Leave the family? And what land were they to go to?

"And will we go?"

His face set uncompromisingly. "Yes."

"But what of Lot?" Sarai couldn't stand the thought of parting from her nephew. After Haran had died, they had taken him into their home, and he had become as a son to them.

"If he wishes, he may come also."

Sarai sucked in a deep breath. How could they just leave their home here and go into some unknown country? She gnawed at her bottom lip. Still, wherever Abram went, she would go also. Life without him didn't bear thinking about. Yet deep inside, she wondered if this God of Abram's would somehow take him away from her. If only she had a son to give him.

"What else did this God say?"

Abram wrapped her in his arms, nuzzling the top of her head with his bearded chin.

"He said, 'I will make you into a great nation, and I will bless you; I will make your name great, and you will be a blessing. I will bless those who bless you, and whoever curses you I will curse, and all peoples on earth will be blessed through you.'"

Sarai trembled in his arms. How could this God make Abram into a mighty nation when he had no offspring? She glanced up at Abram and he met her look squarely.

"I believe Him, Sarai."

She marveled at his faith. It was hard for her to trust in this unknown God, but she knew that she trusted her husband. If he believed, then that was good enough for her. She placed her hands against his cheeks, and lifting herself on her toes, she placed a lingering kiss on his lips. He smiled, and she returned it.

"When do we leave?"

ISAAC AND REBEKAH
Genesis 24

Isaac wandered across the fields near his father's home, his thoughts flitting from one image to another. The sun was descending in the west, sending shadows across the land. He meandered along, searching for something he couldn't put a name to.

His mother had died almost three years ago now, yet the pain was still as intense, the loneliness still as prevalent. Oh, how he missed her!

He was almost forty years old, yet he hadn't found himself a wife to share his life with. For one thing, his father had forbade it. For another, he just wasn't interested in the idol-worshiping Canaanites around him.

Oh, he had nothing against their looks. Many times his eye had been caught by a passing beauty, but they didn't know the Lord. They worshiped stone idols that had no life. Why couldn't they see, as his own father had done, that there was only one true God?

Still, as a man, he had many times been affected by a pair of roving eyes. He wouldn't have been a man if he hadn't, but the feeling was swift and not strong enough to make him forget his allegiance to both his father and his God.

He wondered what the woman would be like

that Eliezer, his father's servant, would return with. Maybe he wouldn't return with a woman at all. What woman in her right mind would leave home and family and travel across miles of desert to marry a man she had never seen? Did he even *want* such a woman?

Still, his father had sent, and Eliezer had gone. Whether things went right or wrong, Eliezer should be returning any day now. It was already long past when they had expected him.

Abraham had been adamant that he, Isaac, should marry within the clan. He wanted no idol worshiper for his son. And yet, who was to say that the women within his clan were followers of the one true God? Had they been so, wouldn't they have followed Abraham when he left Ur and gone with him to seek his God?

He stopped to look around him. He enjoyed visiting with his father, but he needed to get home. Back to Beer Lahai Ro in the south where his home was located. He sighed. What was there for him, anyway? Only more loneliness.

His eyes caught sight of a speck in the distance. Narrowing his look, he waited until the spot grew larger and then turned into a caravan of camels.

Heart suddenly thundering in his chest, he knew with certainty that his wife was about to arrive. He sent a swift prayer heavenward that

Eliezer had chosen wisely.

Taking a deep breath, he went to meet them.

⌒⌒

"Not far now."

Rebekah sighed. That was the same thing Eliezer had said an hour ago. And the hour before that. She fervently hoped that he was right this time. Not for the first time, she wondered what had ever made her agree to this in the first place.

Here she was, miles from her family and friends, about to marry a man she knew nothing about. Well, that was not the case anymore. Eliezer had done nothing but sing the praises of his master, Abraham, and his master's son, Isaac. If Eliezer was to be believed, Abraham was the closest thing to a god that lived on this earth.

What kind of man could inspire such devotion in a servant? Rebekah knew without a doubt that Eliezer would walk through fire to serve his master. It was one of the things that had encouraged her to accept the offer made for her.

And Isaac? What of him? All she really knew was that he had been devoted to his mother and that he was lonely after having lost her.

She twisted the gold bracelets on her wrist, a gift from Abraham. Or had it been Isaac? She would know soon enough. Her stomach tightened at the thought.

All of her life she had heard stories of Abraham

and how he had been called by the one true God to leave his country and go to another. For what reason? Why would God want Abraham to leave his family and his clan, and then seek a wife years later for his son from that same clan? It didn't make much sense to her, but she had to admit that she was fascinated by the man. He had always seemed larger than life to her, and she was anxious to meet him, to see if the stories she had heard were accurate.

Still, she was thankful that she had her nurse, Deborah, with her. To leave family was bad enough, but she could never have parted with Deborah.

Her look settled on each of the maids who had also come with her. What must they be thinking? Were they as frightened as she was? Probably more so.

They ascended a hill and saw spread out before them a vast encampment. Eliezer smiled, his eyes alight with excitement.

"We are home!"

Home. Rebekah breathed in deeply, trying to still the tension throbbing through her body. In the fields to the east she noticed a man walking toward them. This could not be Abraham—he was far too young. His physique showed that he was not unfamiliar with work in the fields. As he drew closer, she could make out the features of his face.

He had a short beard and short brown hair, his skin darkened by the sun. His clothes, though, were not those of a field hand.

She turned to Eliezer. "What man is this that walks in the field to meet us?"

Eliezer smiled broadly. "It is my master."

Realizing that she was about to meet her future husband, Rebekah quickly pulled a veil from the pouch tied to the saddle of the camel and covered herself.

She tapped the camel and it slowly knelt, allowing her to alight. She bowed before Isaac, waiting for him to speak.

⌒‿⌒

Isaac allowed his gaze to wander over the woman bowing before him. He reached down and lifted her to her feet. He could not see her face as yet, but her form was pleasing. He smiled at Eliezer.

"Everything went well, Eliezer?"

Eliezer proceeded to tell him all that had happened in Haran. Isaac's lips parted slightly, his wonder evident. If he had any doubts before of the Lord's leading, they were surely put to rest. It never occurred to him to doubt what Eliezer said. He turned back to Rebekah.

"Welcome," he told her, not sure what else to say.

Eliezer's look went past his shoulder, and he smiled broadly. Isaac turned to find his father coming up behind him. He looked in question at Eliezer, and Eliezer proceeded to tell him all that had transpired. Smiling with satisfaction, Abraham turned to Rebekah.

"Welcome, my daughter. You must be tired after your long journey. Eliezer will show your maids where they might rest." He took her arm. "As for you, come into my tent and tell me all the news of your family." He smiled at Isaac, motioning him to follow.

Isaac stood to the side as his father arranged cushions on the tent floor to accommodate Rebekah. She seated herself gracefully, allowing her veil to drop around her shoulders.

Isaac's mouth parted in surprise. Never had he seen a more beautiful woman. Her hair flowed around her shoulders in a shimmering dark brown mass, light from the brazier giving soft red accents to it. Her skin was a flawless smooth tan, her lips red like the fruit of the pomegranate. She lifted her dark, sultry eyes to his, and he felt his heart stop for an infinitesimal second, then rush on again at an accelerated rate. He could see that his father was just as impressed.

"And how is your family?" Abraham questioned.

Rebekah turned her gaze back to his father, and Isaac felt himself able to breathe again.

"My father died some time ago," she told him. "Perhaps you already knew that?"

Abraham shook his head sadly. "No, I did not."

"My mother and brother are well."

Something in her voice caught Isaac's attention. All was not as well as Rebekah would have them believe. Had she then escaped an abusive situation? He felt his anger rise swiftly, surprised that he should have such a reaction, having known the girl for such a short time. Yet he couldn't deny the fierce possessiveness that rushed through him.

He stood silently while his father continued talking with Rebekah. He was content just to watch her and listen, her voice as melodious as the stringed lyre.

"I will not keep you any longer," Abraham finally said. "I know you must be tired after such a long journey. Isaac will show you to my. . .his mother's tent."

Isaac searched his father's face. He was certain that his father had been about to say "my wife's tent." Even after three years, the pain of his mother's death still showed plainly on his father's features. Why hadn't he realized before that his father had been hurting just as much as he?

Isaac held out a hand to Rebekah. When she placed her own into it, he felt an alarming jolt run through his body. She lifted her eyes to his, and he knew with certainty that he wasn't alone in his feelings.

He pulled her to her feet, reluctantly letting go of her hand.

Rebekah bowed to Abraham, then turned and followed Isaac from the tent.

~ — ~

Isaac held back the flap opening to a large tent. Rebekah preceded him inside, staring curiously around her.

"This was the tent of your mother?" she asked softly.

He nodded. "My father had it set up for you when he sent Eliezer to. . .to find you."

Rebekah remembered her father talking about Abram's connection with the one true God. Had He spoken to Abram—no, she had to remember to call him Abraham—but had God told him that she would be arriving? Eliezer's story of her drawing water from the well in answer to prayer had impressed both her family and herself. Yet did she truly believe in this one God? Her brother Laban hadn't. He still followed the way of the Amorites.

Isaac watched her as she moved around the tent, touching first one item, then another. *Is this the loom that Sarai had woven the tents for her family on?* she wondered. A stone mortar and pestle for grinding grain rested on a small table in the corner. She lifted the pestle from the bowl, then set it down again. Picking up a large goatskin bag, she lifted a brow at Isaac.

"The bag my mother used to churn the butter," he answered her unspoken question. Nodding, she set it beside the grinding bowl on the table.

Rich tapestries hung from the walls of the tent, adding insulation to the strong goat hair walls. They were beautifully wrought, and Rebekah felt a sudden kinship with the woman who had spent so many hours in laboring over them.

She turned to Isaac. "It is a beautiful home. Thank you."

He smiled. "I am pleased you have come," he told her softly, his dark brown eyes assuring her that he spoke more than just words. She felt a stirring inside at his look. He was much older than she, yet he was far more handsome than many men half his age. But then, his mother had been a beautiful woman.

He pulled back the tent flap in preparation for leaving. His eyes met hers once again and something seemed to pass between them.

"I will see you later. Rest."

And then he was gone, and she was left alone with her thoughts. Perhaps there *was* one God after all. She had prayed to this God of Abraham to free her of her brother's tyranny. He had kept a tight rein on her, protecting her from the men around Haran until such time as he was assured of a rich dowry. Eliezer couldn't have come at a better time. Laban's greed had set her free, but he didn't know it. A handsome and wealthy man for a husband. She smiled at her good fortune.

People had been invited from miles around to join in the wedding feast. Isaac had watched all the activity with a great degree of irritation. He would much rather have taken Rebekah as his wife the moment she arrived, but his father had felt the need to celebrate.

Isaac couldn't deny his father this chance at a little cheer. He had been disconsolate for so long that Isaac had begun to worry about him. Now he seemed to have a new lease on life. And all because of Rebekah.

He breathed deeply of the clean air. He loved to tend the sheep, though it was a lonely job. Still, for the past three years he had enjoyed the solitude. Now, however, he was impatient to go back to the camp, and he knew that it was because Rebekah was there.

He saw her walking to join him among the sheep. He smiled a welcome.

"I brought you something to eat," she told him, returning his smile.

He took the packet she handed him, sniffing appreciatively as the smell of fresh-baked bread reached his nose. He unwound the cloth from around the still-warm food.

"You should not have come so far alone," he scolded gently, pleased that she had been willing to do so.

She turned and stared back the way she had just come. She glanced at him in surprise.

"I did not realize I had traveled so far. You can't even see the fields or tents from here."

"I thank you for the food, but please do not come so far unattended again. There are lions in the vicinity."

He saw her pale, glancing furtively around her. He didn't bother to tell her of the ewe he had found slaughtered only that morning. The lioness had come too close to their camp for comfort. It might be necessary to track her down and kill her.

"I did not think. I'm sorry." She looked around her. "Are all these sheep yours?" she asked in surprise.

"No, some of them belong to neighboring families. We share the land."

With sheep, unlike the cattle and goats, he had no concern over proprietorship. Sheep would only answer to one master. When it came time to move them into the sheepfold for the night, he would have no problem identifying his own. Neither would the others who shared this land.

He reached out a hand to Rebekah. "Would you like me to show you around?"

She met his look briefly before casting her eyes to the ground. She placed her hand in his, and, once again, he felt that thrill run through his body. Thank the Lord that his wedding was only two days away. He didn't think he could wait much longer. He had fallen in love with Rebekah the moment he had set eyes on her. But did she feel the same? He would give a lot to know, but unlike facing down a marauding lion, he hadn't the courage to ask.

The sun was beginning to sink toward the west when he finally pulled to a stop. It was time to return to their camp for the night.

He turned to call for the sheep when he noticed movement out of the corner of his eye. A young lioness stood watching from the hill. Her hungry look was fastened on a young lamb that had wandered from its mother's side.

Isaac stood in indecision. They were downwind of the cat, so it had yet to spot them. He needed to protect the herd, but he also needed to protect Rebekah. He heard her sharply indrawn breath and knew that she had spotted the lioness also.

"Isaac. . . ?"

The fear was evident in her voice.

"Listen to me, Rebekah," he told her, never taking his eyes from the lioness. "I want you to slowly head back to the camp. Move slowly and quietly."

She didn't move, and he turned to find her frozen with terror.

"Rebekah," he commanded, "do as I say."

Giving her a slight shove, he turned back to the lioness. He knew the she-cat would not bother with a human if there was easier prey, and right now that prey was the young lamb.

Out of his peripheral vision, he saw Rebekah begin to move away. So intent was the lioness on the lamb, she never even noticed.

Isaac pulled his sling from his belt, then lifted his spear from the ground where he had laid it earlier. He hunched near the ground, trying to make himself as inconspicuous as possible so that he could get near enough to the lion to make a sure shot with his spear. Since she could not scent him, it gave him a slight advantage. He only had the one spear, and if he didn't bring the cat down with the first throw, she could very well turn on him and still rend him to pieces.

When he judged it a safe distance, he leapt to his feet, shouting a cry that rang throughout the countryside around him. As he had expected, the cat froze in panic at the unexpected attack. He threw the spear with enough power that it drove the point clean through the cat. It dropped where it stood, less than fifteen cubits away.

Breathing hard, Isaac tried to calm the racing of his heart and quieten the adrenaline still racing through his veins. Hearing a sound behind him, he turned, ready to do battle with another cat. Instead he saw Rebekah racing to his side.

She threw herself into his arms, weeping copiously. He held her tightly, trying to calm her fears with soothing words of comfort.

"Oh, Isaac! You could have been killed!"

Elation filled him, not so much because of her words, but because of the amount of feeling he could sense behind them. Would she act so if she didn't care for him, at least a little? He somehow didn't think so.

"I am all right," he told her quietly, but it still took some time to hush her tears.

She looked up at him through tear-drenched eyes. Something he saw there brought more hope to his heart.

"Do you love me, Rebekah?" he finally dared to ask.

"How can you ask me such a thing?" she asked angrily. She thumped his chest with a small fist. "Have I not tried to tell you so for the past three days?"

Isaac thought back on the time they had spent together over the past week. Yes, there had been something different about her attitude the last three days, but he had attributed it to nervousness over the upcoming nuptials.

He studied her face closely. How could he have missed the love shining out of her eyes? For Isaac, that was enough. He pulled her close and kissed her with the intensity of his own feelings.

She returned his kisses in like manner, the two sharing things that had yet to be said in words.

Isaac praised God for this wonderful gift of love that had come to him in a desperate time. He praised his father for having the faith to trust in the one true God, and teaching him to do the same. He praised Rebekah for her courage in daring to take the same risk his own father had taken so many years ago.

Well could he understand Abraham's joy for him. The joy of a love that would know no bounds. Hadn't his father been given the same blessing?

With a call to the sheep, he let Rebekah go, and taking her hand, they made their way back to where he knew Abraham awaited them.

JOSEPH AND ASENATH
GENESIS 37–45

From a pit in the earth, to a slave's quarters at Potiphar's, to another pit in the earth, and now to the palace of Pharaoh himself. Joseph shook his head slightly, still unable to believe it all. He looked around him at the lavish quarters that were now his own and sighed. Truly Yahweh's works were beyond comprehension.

He leaned upon the parapet surrounding the balcony that extended over the inner courtyard below. Twisting Pharaoh's signet ring that the great man had placed there himself, Joseph marveled at his good fortune. The warm breeze feathered across his face and he leaned into it, enjoying the freedom he had missed for the last two years. Although it had been several months since he had been brought to the palace, he still had a hard time accepting his latest circumstances.

Movement below caught his eye. A woman was crossing the courtyard, heading for the door that led to the inner palace. Instant recognition sent him swiftly across the room and to the door that led to the hallway. Jerking open the portal, he commanded one of the guards standing sentry, "The courtyard. Bring Lady Asenath to me."

He retreated back into his room, his emotions roiling. It had been two years since he had last seen Asenath, but the pictures in his mind of that time were as clear as though they were yesterday.

It was only moments later that the guard preceded Asenath into the room. Joseph nodded for him to leave them alone. When the door closed behind the guard, Joseph was finally able to look at the woman standing with head bent down.

"Asenath," he breathed softly.

"My Lord Zaphenath-Paneah," she responded without ever looking up.

She was beautiful, her dark hair swinging softly around her shoulders, the soft white of her linen dress clinging to her body. Joseph went closer and, lifting her face with his cupped palm, told her, "I am Joseph to you."

She lifted her eyes to meet his, and he saw the burning anger there, turning the dark brown of her orbs to an almost obsidian. It had been two years, but still she had not forgiven him.

"That name means nothing to me. Someone by that name betrayed me years ago."

Joseph felt his own anger kindle. "I never betrayed you."

She pulled from his touch. "No," she agreed, her voice harsh with concealed fury. "That is true. We never had an understanding between us. It was my father you betrayed."

"I never betrayed your father," he told her inflexibly.

Something flickered in her eyes that passed so quickly Joseph couldn't fathom it. She turned away from him, but grasping her forearm, he turned her back.

"Are you saying my mother lied?" she snapped.

"I am not saying anything except that I did not betray either you *or* your father."

Tears started in her eyes. "What do you want from me? Absolution?"

Joseph touched her cheek with gentle fingers. He brushed her dark bangs to the side, his look intense. "I want us to be friends again."

Her lips pressed into a tight line. "Whatever you command, my lord."

He wrapped firm fingers around her forearms, his own eyes darkening to match hers. "It is not a command, Asenath."

She placed her palms against his chest, and he felt his heart rate accelerate. There was no softening in her look.

"It does not matter. My father has been made priest of On, and we will be leaving the city soon."

Joseph's lips parted in surprise. "Leaving?"

The tears that had been merely hinted at now started a path down her cheeks. "He could not face you as second in command to Pharaoh."

His look roamed her face. "More likely he

could not face himself."

Asenath shoved against him, but he didn't release her. "There you go again, accusing my father of something."

Pulling her over to a couch, he forced her to sit. When he seated himself beside her, she moved to put some distance between them.

"Think about it, Asenath. You are an intelligent woman. If your father believed what your mother had said, why would he have sent me to prison instead of slaying me on the spot? And why put me in prison under his own command?"

Confusion furrowed her brow momentarily before the anger returned to wipe it away. "Because he *loved* you! He trusted you!"

Joseph leaned forward to look into her eyes. "Why?"

She jumped to her feet and strode to the balcony. Joseph followed.

"How can you believe such a thing of me?" he asked. "Especially after what we have shared."

She turned, leaning back against the balustrade. Her fingers clutched the stone until they shone white, matching the color of her wraparound dress. When she lifted her face to meet his, the gold headpiece that she wore reflected the bright sunlight, momentarily blinding him.

"May I leave now?" she demanded.

He wanted to tell her no, but he realized that

right now it would be futile to reason with her further. He must give her time to think about what he had said. He sighed heavily.

"Yes."

When she would have passed him, he reached out and caught her arm. "Can you *really* believe such a thing of me?"

Her lips parted slightly. "I don't know," she whispered. "I really don't know."

He released her and watched her cross the room to disappear from his sight seconds later. Unlike the last time, he would not allow her to be parted from him again.

⌒‿⌒

Asenath sat before her dressing table, staring at herself in the polished silver mirror that hung on the wall. She did not see the glowing beauty of her dark black tresses, shimmering brown eyes, or full painted lips. Her mind was far away, in the past.

Lifting the jar of cream from the table, she began to remove the kohl from her eyes and the red ochre clay from her lips and cheeks. Still, her mind was not on what she was doing. She was remembering when Joseph had first come to their home. He had been only seventeen years of age, but even at that young age, his beauty of body put many of even her father's strongest guards to shame.

She had been only ten at the time, but from

the moment she had laid eyes on him, she had loved him. There was something charismatic about Joseph. He attracted without meaning to.

She got up from the table and went into the garden just outside her room. The fragrance from the lotus blossoms drifted to her on the soft night breeze. A servant followed with a palm leaf fan, not so much to cool her as to keep away the mosquitoes.

She sat on the side of the pool, watching the fish dart through the water at her intrusion. Running her fingers through the water, she remembered the last time she had been here with Joseph. That had been over two years ago. She had found him in the garden, cleaning the tiles around the pool.

They had talked together for quite some time, mostly about his God. Asenath found this God of Joseph's fascinating. Especially when he had told her the story of his dreams. Here in Egypt dreamers were held in high regard, especially when they turned out to be prophets.

She had believed everything Joseph had told her. Until that terrible day. Frustrated, she turned to the eunuch who attended her.

"Leave me, Asad."

He bowed low, leaving her to her churning thoughts. She returned to her room, dousing the lamps and crawling into her bed. The silk sheets were cool and comforting, at least to her body. Her mind, however, refused to be soothed.

Was it true what Joseph said? Had her mother lied to them all? She couldn't believe it, and yet Joseph had shown himself to be honorable in every way. Her father had trusted him with everything because he had proved himself so honest.

Asenath's face flushed warmly when she remembered the time she had thrown herself at him. There had been an attraction there, she knew. She could see it in his eyes. Still, he had gently rebuffed her. It said something for Joseph that they had been able to remain friends even after that act.

Today she had seen that same attraction in his eyes, but this time she had the sure conviction that he would not back away. Her heart began to thump erratically when she remembered the darkening of his eyes and the huskiness of his voice.

Joseph. For two years now he had been gone from her life, but she had never forgotten him. And now he wanted to be her friend again. How on this earth could he ever believe that would be possible?

❧ ⎯ ❧

Asenath sat on the side of the pool, watching the fish swim to and fro. The morning sun had yet to reach intensity, and she was enjoying the time before the heat would force her to retreat inside.

She took off her papyrus sandals and slid her feet into the cooling water, laughing as the fish darted away.

Her cat, Tivat, jumped to the edge of the tiles, swatting at the frantically circling fish.

"Tivat, you know that those fish are not for you to eat," she rebuked.

The cat blinked at her before joining her, his soft black fur rubbing silkily against her arm. She rubbed his head, causing a rumble to begin deep in his chest.

"Now this is a picture I remember well."

Startled by the deep voice, Asenath came to her feet, Tivat hissing his displeasure against the sudden move.

"Joseph!"

A slow smile spread across his face, sending Asenath's heart rate to racing like a speeding chariot. Realizing that she was still without her daily makeup, Asenath colored hotly with embarrassment. The smile on Joseph's face increased.

"You needn't be embarrassed. I have seen you without your makeup before." He reached to the side, plucking a red flower from the bush beside him and then placing it gently above her ear. "In fact, I have always preferred you this way."

The color in her cheeks deepened. "You jest."

"Not so. I love to see the color of your eyes. They remind me of a beautiful golden topaz."

He was too close. She moved to put some distance between them. "You know as well as I that the eye makeup is necessary to protect our eyes from the sun and sand that cause the eye diseases."

He nodded his head in affirmation. "Still, you are beautiful as you are."

His words threatened her composure more than a little bit.

"What are you doing here?" she asked, her voice coming out more breathless than she intended.

"I have come to see your father."

A rush of alarm swept through her. In his position as second to Pharaoh, Joseph could have her father executed if he so chose.

"He is not here. He has already made the trip to On with my mother. I will be joining them in a few days, after we have finished seeing to things here."

He came and stood in front of her, so close that she could feel the heat emanate from his body. There was no way to escape him. If she stepped backward even an inch, she would find herself in the garden pool. The look she fixed upon him brought a swift frown to his face.

"Are you afraid of me, Asenath?"

Was she? Or was she afraid of the effect he had on her?

Instead of answering his question, she asked

one of her own. "Why did you wish to speak with my father?"

He opened his mouth to speak, then closed his lips against the words. He turned away from her, watching the servants as they carried items from the garden to be packed with the other belongings being sent to On.

"That is between him and me," he finally answered. He smiled to take the sting from the words, but Asenath wasn't reassured.

"I have my chariot outside. Come for a ride with me."

Asenath cast her look to the ground even as she felt her cheeks heat. "Is that a command, my lord?"

She heard his deep sigh. "It is a request."

Glancing up, she realized that she really wanted to go with him. "I still have no makeup on," she demurred.

His slow smile sent her pulse rate soaring. "One day will not make a difference." He held out his hand. "Come."

She placed her hand within his and felt a jolt run through her entire body. She met his look and knew that he had felt it, too. Was he remembering that kiss that they had shared in this very garden so many years ago? His smile turned into a full-fledged grin, and she knew that he was. Her doubts about him were flitting away like the butterfly flying over the garden wall. She was very much afraid that there would be no turning back.

⌒─ ─⌒

Joseph never tired of racing across the desert sands in his chariot. To feel the wind blasting against his face reminded him that he was free. Feeling Asenath's uneasy shiver, he slowed the horses to a walk and turned them back toward the great river.

He pulled to a stop at the water's edge. Already the Nile River was in its flooding season, sending life-giving water across much of the land.

He leaned against the front of the chariot so that he could better see Asenath's face. She tilted her head slightly, returning his look.

"I have thought of you so often," he told her softly.

She pulled slightly away from him, at least as much as the chariot would allow.

"Joseph. . .don't."

He turned her to face him, his hands wrapping warmly around her forearms. His look was intense.

"Asenath, I never betrayed your father. You have got to believe that."

She bit her lip, her confusion evident. "Why would my mother lie?"

"Your mother is a lonely woman. She is young and still lovely. When your father agreed to be made a eunuch to serve Pharaoh, he could not have realized what that would mean for your mother."

She tried to step out of the chariot, but he wouldn't allow it. "Asenath, I don't care who else believes me, but it's important to me that *you* do."

"Why?" she demanded, her eyes dark and stormy.

"I think you know why." He moved his hands slowly up and down her arms. "I want to tell you about a dream I had."

She turned her back to him. "Please, Joseph. Don't."

"It was about you and me," he continued, as though she hadn't interrupted, "and our two sons."

He heard her sharp intake of breath. "No. I don't believe you." Her almond-shaped eyes were full of pleading. "Please, Joseph. Take me home."

He could no more resist that plea than he could deny the dream he spoke of. She obviously needed more time to sort things out in her mind, but he knew with certainty that one day she would be his. Joseph sighed heavily, letting her go and lifting the reins. "As you wish."

⌒──⌒

Asenath stood before Pharaoh, wondering at his summons. She tried to keep her eyes from straying to Joseph standing at his right side, but it was a losing battle. She had never seen him looking so tense.

"Asenath," Pharaoh intoned, "I am giving you to Zaphenath-Paneah as his wife."

Asenath's almond eyes opened wide. She glanced at Joseph, but his expression was inscrutable. Had this been his idea?

Pharaoh smiled at her beatifically, as though he had just granted her some large favor. She supposed it would be considered that way to most, but she had other ideas. Still, one didn't argue with Pharaoh. She kept any words of censure to herself.

Pharaoh motioned her forward, and she moved forward on unsteady legs. When he joined her hand with Joseph's, her whole body started to tremble. Joseph noticed, sending her messages of reassurance with his eyes.

She couldn't remember what happened afterward or even leaving the throne room, but she soon found herself in the palace gardens. Joseph finally stopped and turned her to face him.

"I'm sorry," he told her softly. "Somehow Pharaoh found out how I feel about you. He thought he was doing me a favor."

"And you?" she asked. "Do you object?"

He studied her several long seconds before he spoke. "I have no objections. And you?"

She moved away from him, dipping her hand into the cool waters of the lotus pond. She thought back to that day several weeks ago when she had searched out her father to ascertain the truth from him. He had been preparing to go to the temple and dress and feed the statue of Atum. His smile of welcome had almost deterred her, but she had to know the truth.

"Father, I wished to ask you something."

He carefully checked the fruit in the basket that would be offered to the god. "Ask then."

Asenath wet suddenly dry lips. "Why did you not have Joseph killed when he attacked Mother? Why did you just send him to prison, and under your own guard?"

Her father stilled his movements. When he turned to her, there was anger in his eyes. "We will not discuss this."

She was not to be thwarted. "I have to know, Father."

He didn't miss the intensity of her look. He gave a long, protracted sigh. "I see." He shook his head. "I did not miss the growing feelings between you two. I think I would have welcomed Joseph as a suitor had he been anything but a slave."

Asenath flushed. She hadn't realized that her own feelings had been so obvious, though she shouldn't have been surprised.

"You don't believe he did it, do you?"

A look of guilt passed across his features. "I could not deny your mother, especially in front of other servants."

Asenath felt the world reeling around her. "But you don't believe he did it," she breathed, horrified at the thought that she had never given Joseph a chance to explain.

Her father could not meet her horrified look.

"And you let him sit in prison for two years!"

"May the gods forgive me," he whispered brokenly.

"May Joseph's God forgive you!" she retorted in return.

Joseph's touch brought her back to the present. His worried frown brought a small smile to her face.

"I talked to my father," she told him, and saw him tense. "Can you ever forgive me for doubting you, Joseph?" she asked softly.

He looked at her in surprise, her words finally registering. Taking a deep breath, he pulled her into his arms.

"Asenath," he breathed.

She wrapped her arms around his waist. "Oh, Joseph. I *will* be your wife."

When his lips descended on hers, she knew that her dreamer had been right. His God was truly an awesome God. She looked forward to the years ahead, to having Joseph's sons. Her dreamer had finally come home.

MOSES AND ZIPPORAH
EXODUS 2

The stars shone brightly in the dark night sky as Zipporah stared out over plains made shadowy by the light of a full moon. A warm night breeze sent strands of dark hair blowing across her face. She pushed them behind her ear, glad that she had left her head covering in the tent. She loved the feel of the warm air as it caressed her skin.

It had been only three days since the stranger from Egypt had entered their lives, yet somehow she knew that with that advent, her life would never be the same again.

He was strong and virile, to be sure, but there was something about Moses that suggested greatness, a greatness that had yet to be realized.

"Shalom."

Startled, Zipporah turned to find the object of her mind's wanderings mere feet away. Knowing that he could not read her thoughts did nothing to keep the flush from warming her cheeks.

He came and stood next to her, his look tracing the same path as her own. His gaze came back to rest on her.

"It's a beautiful night."

Zipporah agreed. "Elohim has certainly favored us with a perfect time and a perfect place."

She could feel the intensity of his look. "The God of the Hebrews."

It was more a question than a statement. Zipporah's eyes met his, the firelight from the tents behind them giving his brown orbs a luminosity that left Zipporah strangely affected.

"There is only one God," she told him softly.

This man dressed like an Egyptian and spoke like one, yet he had not the appearance of one. It was obvious that his beard had been a recent acquisition, more evidence of his being Egyptian, yet his bone structure looked more like her own people. And yet when he had chased off the shepherds who had accosted her and her sisters, he had fought like one trained in the art of war. She was extremely curious about him.

He smiled wryly. "And is that not the temple of Hathor that I see in the distance?"

Even here in Midian, some distance from Egypt itself, the Egyptian presence could be felt. Egyptian slaves mined the copper that was in the red sandstone rocks, along with the beautiful turquoise stones that were to be found here. Even her own father had made considerable wealth from the copper industry. It didn't surprise her that Moses recognized the Egyptian goddess of mining, but it greatly increased her curiosity.

"Who are you, Moses?" she asked suddenly and saw the quick veil that shadowed his features.

He glanced down at her briefly before returning his gaze once more to the temple that seemed so close but was, in reality, far off in the Timna Valley.

"I'm a man, Zipporah. Nothing else."

She knew she should respect his silence, but her curiosity yearned for satisfaction. Her father had told her often that it was her greatest failing.

"You dress like an Egyptian, but you aren't one, are you?"

The look he gave her would have quelled a lesser individual. She continued to stare at him silently, yet her very silence demanded an answer. He heaved a great sigh, one corner of his mouth turning up wryly.

"There's nothing quite as resolute as a woman's curiosity, is there?"

She should have felt embarrassed, but she returned his half smile with a full one of her own. He sighed again, smiling, the soft summer breeze ruffling the bangs of his Egyptian haircut.

"I have already told your father my story, so I suppose I might as well tell you, also."

Zipporah listened to his story in growing wonder. The sense of his impending greatness grew with each word. It was obvious that the Lord had watched over this child of Abraham, had even led him to this land, but for what purpose?

He hesitated slightly before admitting to

killing an Egyptian guard.

"And now Pharaoh wants you dead?" she asked, appalled.

He started slightly as though he had just remembered her presence. Turning to her once again, he shrugged. "It's the law."

She wanted to know more, but he turned the conversation with finality.

"And you, Zipporah? Why would the daughter of a prince be out watering the sheep? Surely that is a job for servants."

She was not offended at the obvious rebuke. "My father believes everyone should be useful, not just decorative. Besides, the sheep are our livelihood. Who would look after them better?"

He nodded his agreement. "True."

They both settled into silence, yet the lack of conversation didn't bother Zipporah. The silence was a friendly one, comfortable.

Zipporah ambled toward the oasis pool at the edge of the camp, and Moses fell into step beside her.

"Tell me about your Hebrew God," he requested.

Zipporah stared at him in surprise. "Did not your mother teach you about Him?"

"My Hebrew mother taught me of Him, yes. But my Egyptian mother also taught me about the Egyptian gods. I know more about them than this one you call Elohim."

Seating herself next to the pool, Zipporah wondered just where to begin. When Moses' look fixed on her with such intensity, her mouth went dry and her heart started to thrum in an irregular manner. Yes, she could picture this man as a prince of Egypt. There was absolutely nothing servile about him.

She finally began by telling him of God's calling of Abraham out of the land of Haran.

Moses watched Zipporah while she tended the sheep. Egyptians considered sheep the lowest kind of animal, while Hebrews tended them lovingly. It was not the first time that he noticed such differences between his two peoples.

Yet though he had been raised a prince of Egypt, he had always felt separate. Knowing his Hebrew heritage probably had something to do with it. More likely it had to do with the resentment of the Egyptian people.

He had heard the tale of Pharaoh's sacred scribe trying to slay him when Thermuthis, his Egyptian mother, had presented him to Pharaoh. The scribe had predicted that Moses would overthrow the kingdom of Egypt. The Egyptians mistrusted him, and the Hebrews were looking to him for something he wasn't certain he could give. The one time he had tried to help his people had ended in disaster.

Moses shook his head to rid it of such thoughts. He had no desire to be king of Egypt, and he was glad that he had left Egypt and Goshen far behind. Having found peace here among the Bedouins, he was content.

His thoughts came back to Zipporah. What would she say when she found out that her father had agreed to give her to Moses as his wife? Would she find it acceptable?

Her ideas of this Hebrew God left him confused, but then that had been true most of his life. The Hebrews had only one God. Even Zipporah's father's name, Reuel, meant "friend of God." But which god?

He lifted his eyes to the bright afternoon sun. The Egyptians had many gods, but none more powerful than Ra, the sun god, giver of life. Even the temple of Hathor he could see in the distance was only one of many. How was he to ever be certain what was true and right? If he searched with all of his heart and mind, would it then be made clear to him? And how should he go about searching? And for that matter *why* should he?

Something told him he might find the truth here among the Bedouins. They lived so close to the land, and looking around him at the diversity of the landscape, he couldn't doubt the existence of divinity.

The swaying palm trees around him fed by a

hidden water source, the shifting sands beyond, the rising mountains in the distance—all of these things spoke to his heart, his soul.

His look returned to Zipporah. He had been married once before. Tharbis was an Ethiopian princess, and although she had loved him, for him the marriage had been to fulfill a vow. It had been more a political alliance, and although he had grieved her death as one would grieve over a friend, his heart had remained intact.

When Zipporah looked up and caught his eye, he felt a rush of heat surge through his body that had nothing whatever to do with the sun. He had an uncanny premonition that his life was never going to be the same again, and he knew that a great part of that would have to do with this woman.

"Your father wishes to speak with you," he called out.

Nodding, she yelled for one of her sisters to take her place at the head of the herd. She joined Moses and together they walked the distance back to the camp, each making light conversation.

Moses found himself making comparisons between Zipporah and his first wife. Although Zipporah's skin was dark, it was nothing like Tharbis's. And Zipporah's hair was long and shiny, its darkness emphasized by the olive oil used to condition it, unlike Tharbis's, which was short and curly, though much the same color. Tharbis had been an ethereal beauty, whereas Zipporah could only be described as earthy, not really a beauty, but still pleasing to the eye.

It was in the personalities that their paths diverged. It was hard to explain, even to himself. Tharbis had been energetic and exciting, and although Zipporah could claim that same energy, as was evidenced by her defense of the herd against the male shepherds, there was something calming, almost hypnotic about her.

She met his look briefly and he felt again that warm rush of feeling. Did she feel anything similar? The color that rushed to her cheeks told him that she felt something, but that could be embarrassment, or shyness, alone. Frankly, his heart quailed at the thought of her reaction to her father's proposal.

⌒──⌒

Zipporah blinked her long, dark lashes several times and swallowed hard. All girls dreamed of love, yet few were given the opportunity to find it before they were given in marriage. It said something for her father's patience that he had waited until now to give her away. Most women were married shortly after they came into womanhood, but her father had accepted her rejections of suitors until she was now seventeen years of age.

The look in her father's eyes told her this

one would not be rejected. She glanced at Moses and met his intent regard. Swallowing again, she looked back at her father. How could he choose a man for her who worshiped foreign gods? Reuel, friend of God. How was this possible?

If looks were anything to go by, she had no objection. Moses was by far the most handsome man she had ever seen. His courtesy and manners she also had no complaints against. But this manner of questioning God, that really bothered her. Still. . .

"I. . .I have no objection, Father."

Reuel smiled widely. He looked at Moses standing patiently behind Zipporah.

"Let us make the arrangements."

❧ ⎯ ❧

Zipporah seated herself beside her father where he reclined next to the fire. For a brief moment he had no demands on his time, but she knew that wouldn't last very long, so she tried to gather her thoughts into some kind of order to approach him.

He glanced at her from the side of his eyes. "You have something you wish to say, my daughter?"

She reached out to retrieve a stick that hadn't quite made it into the fire. Twisting it through her fingers, she tried to decide how best to begin.

"You have always taught us that it was important to marry within the clan."

"That is so."

Zipporah watched him studying the fire. She frowned, recognizing the look on his face. She may have started this conversation, but he was definitely leading it.

"Moses is not of our clan."

"He is not of our tribe, but he is definitely from our clan."

Confused, she threw the stick into the fire and turned fully to face him. "How is that so?"

"Moses is from the tribe of Levi, and therefore can be reckoned within the clan of Abraham. Although we are from Midian, Abraham's son by Keturah, we are still children of Abraham."

Zipporah nodded, seeing where he was leading. He looked at her more fully, and she noticed the gleam in his eyes.

"I have had a vision, Zipporah, and it has to do with Moses."

A chill ran through her body. As a priest of God, her father had had visions before, but they were not usually welcome ones. She held her breath waiting for him to continue.

"The time has come for Elohim to keep His promise to Father Abraham."

⌒～⌒

"A little more to the right."

Heart thundering with apprehension, Moses did as Zipporah suggested and swung her body farther to the right. He tightened his grip on her legs as his own feet dug for a grip in the rock-hard ground. His stomach muscles bunched against the earth, his arm muscles straining against Zipporah's suspended weight. He gritted his teeth, the sweat pouring from his forehead. How had she ever managed to talk him into this, anyway?

"I've got him!"

The jubilant voice caused him to instantly retract Zipporah from the edge of the rocky face where she had been dangling moments before. Pulling the lamb from her arms, he unceremoniously dropped it to the side before reaching for Zipporah.

"Are you all right? Praise Elohim that you didn't break your neck!"

His hands lightly touched her arms where she had sustained severe scrapes and bruises. He shook his head.

"Never again! I will never again let you talk me into something so foolhardy," he rasped, his heart only now slowing to a steady beat.

She rolled to her back, grinning at him unrepentantly. "You know it was the only way."

Exasperated, he got to his feet, pulling her up after him. She stumbled into his arms, and he smiled broadly at her startled face. Instead of releasing her, he wrapped his arms more securely around her. Although she placed her palms against his chest, she didn't resist him. Cocking her head to the side, she smiled slyly.

"Had you not been with me, I still would have managed it on my own."

He didn't doubt it for a second. The woman was without fear. He stared hard into her eyes.

"In three days' time you will be my wife. Then perhaps I will have a little more control of you."

Instead of being offended, she grinned saucily. "I would not count on that too much, my lord."

She was right, and he knew it. He might as well tame the great sea as to try and tame her. Which was probably what drew him so intensely. Although she was gentle and serene most of the time, she could be as hard as iron at others. She was an enigma that he never tired of trying to solve.

In much less time than it had taken to cross the great desert by foot, he had fallen in love with Zipporah. Now, he had only to make her fall in love with him.

◦——◦

Zipporah couldn't help but notice Moses' increased attention. Her objections to him had faded ever so slowly as he overcame them one by one.

He had turned into a devoted worshiper of the Lord as he spent time among them. She couldn't doubt his sincerity, but neither could she ignore his reserve. He believed in Elohim, but he hadn't quite given up the old gods he had known for so many years.

Now, here she was on her wedding day, wondering just how far his interest in her extended. His gaze wandered over the white embroidered tunic she was wearing and a gleam entered his eyes. When he looked at her as he was looking at her now, she knew that she could deny him nothing. Whatever her doubts, they didn't include her love for him. It had grown slowly as she had gotten to know him, and now it had settled into her heart with finality.

When her father wrapped a gold cord around their wrists to bind them together, she knew that she had received a blessing far greater than she deserved. It was not often that a woman was able to marry for love.

Moses looked into her eyes, and her heart almost stopped beating. For the first time, he allowed his love for her to show. She could hardly believe that it could be true, but there was no denying what she saw in the dark brown depths of his eyes. As though he realized her need for confirmation, he spoke softly.

"I love you, Zipporah."

She gladly went into his arms then, and he held her tightly. He tilted her chin to see her face, waiting for her answer. There was only one that she could give.

"Oh, Moses. I love you, too."

Whatever Elohim had in store for them, she knew that they could face it together.

RAHAB AND SALMON
Joshua 2–6

Rahab stood on a hill, staring at the smoldering rubble that had once been the great city of Jericho, and felt an overwhelming sense of guilt mixed with relief. She had saved her family and herself, but she had betrayed her people. She tried to summon the anger that had led her to this point, but it would not come. Only intense grief.

She brushed a dark brown ringlet of hair away from her face. Her normally energetic honey-colored eyes were dull with fatigue and worry.

For years she had lived in that city, a slave to any man's passion and lust, but no more. She hadn't regretted her decision to live the life of a prostitute. It had been necessary to save her family, the only people who meant anything in the world to her.

In an act of betrayal by one of her "customers," she had been about to lose her home and everything she owned. She shouldn't have been surprised by Anek's duplicity, but she was. Her anger against Anek had spilled over until it had consumed her waking thoughts, and many of her sleeping ones, as well.

All of that had been pushed to the back of her mind when news of the Israelites had reached her ears. Unlike the people of her city, she had no faith in the great walls that surrounded her. From what she had heard, those walls stood no chance against a God who could part the Red Sea—a God who could defeat the kings Sihon and Og.

Many rumors had come to her about the Israelites, but the one that frightened her most was the fact that they stoned prostitutes to death. She had never regretted her life before, but one look into Salmon's eyes had brought guilt such as she had never felt.

When Salmon and Isaachar had come to her house, she had known that they were spies. One couldn't be in the business she was in and not know something about men. It was at that moment that the idea born of intense anger had come to her, the idea that would save her family and yet destroy her city.

Although she had won a promise from the two spies to save herself and her family, the look of loathing that had come with it had left her mortified. She snorted slightly. It was easy for them to condemn. This God of theirs had made provisions for women left destitute, but her own people were not as caring. The gods of this land were as cold as the stone they were carved from.

"Rahab."

Rahab turned to find her mother standing behind her. Her look went past Rahab's shoulder to the view beyond, and tears started in her eyes.

"What's to become of us now?"

Shrugging her shoulders, Rahab turned and began walking back to their camp. The Israelites had provided them with a tent, but little else. At least they had shelter from the coming rain.

"Does it matter, Mother? At least we have the provisions we brought with us and the gold I had hidden away. Besides, we are alive. What is more important than that?"

When they reached the camp, her crippled father looked at her with despairing eyes, but he remained silent. Not so her brother Jezer.

"It would be best if we left these Israelites to themselves and found refuge among one of the other cities close by."

Rahab's smile was without mirth. "Don't you understand yet? There is nowhere in this land that you can leave the Hebrews behind. Their God has given them this land, and no one can stand in His way."

Her other brother, Kuruk, stepped forward. "Are you saying that you mean to stay with them?"

Rahab remembered the look from the two spies. Although Isaachar's was one of intense loathing, Salmon's had been more of disappointment. "I doubt if they will allow it."

"Then let us decide where we shall go," Jezer decided.

Irritated, Rahab glared at them all. If not for her, they would all be dead by now, and now her brothers wanted to take control. Still, she couldn't understand her own reluctance to leave a people who so obviously despised her.

So intent was Rahab on their discussion, she failed to hear the approaching footsteps. When her brother's look went past her shoulder, she turned to find the spy, Salmon, standing behind her. Standing next to him was a man older in age but just as magnificent in stature. There was no doubting that this was the man Joshua that Salmon had told her was their leader.

"You are welcome to stay with our camp, or you are free to leave," Joshua told them.

Before Rahab could reply, Kuruk stepped forward and spoke for them. "We will be leaving in the morning."

Rahab glanced at Salmon and found his look fixed on her. She couldn't read what was in his eyes, but the magnetic pull of them held her spellbound. Was he remembering their conversation about his God, or was he perhaps thinking of her past profession?

She recognized the look in his eyes, having seen it many times before. He found her attractive, though by his rigid stance she doubted it was a welcome feeling.

Her own response to the man had been

unusual, to say the least. What was there about him that made her squirm with regret over her chosen profession? When she looked into his serious brown eyes, she wished that she could face him without her past to separate them. But the past could not be undone, and regrets would get one nowhere.

"As you wish," Joshua stated. He turned and left, Salmon hesitating slightly before following.

Rahab watched them go with a feeling akin to panic. Her mind was in total confusion. The words Salmon had spoken to her about his God and the positive proof of His existence that was still burning behind her made her want to know more.

"Come, Rahab," her mother called. "We need to prepare for our journey tomorrow."

With even greater reluctance than before, she turned to do as she was bidden.

⌒──⌒

Salmon stared broodingly into the campfire. He hadn't been able to get thoughts of Rahab out of his mind from the moment he had met her. Though disgusted with her profession, he thought he understood. Her willingness to do whatever it took to save her family said much in her favor. Still. . .

Joshua seated himself next to Salmon. He studied Salmon a moment before turning his gaze to the fire.

"There is something bothering you, Salmon?"

"No, sir," Salmon denied.

Joshua turned his look back on Salmon, a slow smile curving his lips. "The harlot is a fine-looking woman."

Salmon cringed. He hated that word. *Harlot.*

"You have the right by conquest to have her if you so wish."

Heart thumping wildly, Salmon turned his stare on the older man. "What are you saying?"

Joshua stood, brushing the sand from his clothes. "Nothing, only a reminder."

When Joshua entered his own tent, Salmon got up and walked to edge of their camp. He stood silently, moodily watching the small fire in the distance until that fire disappeared.

⌒──⌒

Rahab walked along the edge of the swollen Jordan River. The waters rushed by in a torrent. She shook her head. Only a powerful God could have caused such waters to stop flowing long enough to allow the Israelites to cross its mighty path.

It was not yet totally light, she having wakened long before the others. Restless, she had decided to go for a walk. Unwise perhaps with the Israelites so near, but at this point she didn't really care. She was numb, devoid of feeling. Even her ability to reason and make judgments seemed to have left her.

She heard a horn blow loudly in the distance and assumed that it was the Israelite call to wake the camp. It seemed somewhat early to her, but what did she know having lived in a city all her life.

Moments later she heard a small, dim cry. It seemed to be coming from the river. All manner of thoughts went racing through her mind, leaving her limp with fear.

Seconds later she spotted what was making the noise. A small child clung tenaciously to a rock some distance in the river. The rushing water pounded the little boy, submerging his head from time to time. He would not be able to hold on much longer.

Without thinking, Rahab plunged into the water, its coldness taking her breath away. She fought to keep her footing. Although she had learned how to swim as a child, the raging waters were more than she thought she could handle.

Inevitably, she was swept off her feet and carried swiftly downstream. She struggled against the wild current, trying to make her way back toward the rock where the child was still clinging.

In horror, she saw the boy plucked from the rock and sent tumbling toward her. Swimming with all her might, she was able to make it to the spot where the child would pass in seconds.

She grabbed the boy's tunic as he was swept

past, and together the two of them went swirling farther downstream.

Holding on to the child with one arm, Rahab kicked strongly, moving them eventually toward the bank and safety.

Her sodden clothes weighing her down, Rahab struggled to get them both farther onto the shore. She sat down next to the child, her breathing ragged with effort. Pushing the wet hair from her eyes, she turned the small boy over and felt near his neck for signs of life. A reassuring rhythm moved against her fingers.

Rolling the boy to his stomach, she pushed down hard on his back. After several times she was rewarded when he coughed and spit up the water he had taken into his lungs. She rolled him to his back again, checking him for injuries.

As the child became more aware of his surroundings, he hesitantly smiled up at her, and her heart turned over. He reminded her of her own nephew, Asser, whom she loved above all others.

"Are you all right?" she asked.

He nodded slightly, his curious brown eyes giving back look for look. Rahab leaned her head against her hand. Now that she was safe, her strength was beginning to fail. The landscape began to tilt and twirl around her.

The last thing she could remember before falling into unconsciousness was a loud voice shouting, pounding horses' hooves, and strong arms lifting her from the ground.

～――～

Salmon pushed the tent flap aside and entered the dim interior. He saw his sister sitting close to the pallet where Rahab lay, still unconscious.

"How is she?"

Pisgah nodded. "I see color returning to her face. She should be fine."

Salmon released the breath he hadn't realized he had been holding. "Thank the Lord."

His sister turned to answer him, but Rahab's slight stirring turned her attention back to the mat.

"She is awakening."

They both watched as Rahab's eyes fluttered, the lids lifting ever so slowly. Confusion gave way to understanding when she noticed Salmon standing near.

"It was you who picked me up?" she questioned.

He nodded. Thinking of that moment still made his heart race like mad. "Do you remember what happened?"

"There was a boy."

"My nephew. You saved his life." When he had been made aware of the child's disappearance, he had blown his horn to give the emergency signal. Men had tumbled from their tents, their spears and swords ready for battle. It had taken some time to get his message through to everyone of the boy missing. He had climbed on his horse with others doing the same and gone searching. They had seen from the hill as Rahab had been swept downstream, young Caleb shortly behind her.

Pisgah spoke then, and Salmon could tell that Rahab didn't understand the Hebrew language. He spoke in Chaldean. "My sister says that we can never repay you for saving her son. Whatever we have is yours."

Rahab looked at Pisgah. She wet her lips and smiled. "Tell her I would like her friendship."

His sister looked at him questioningly. He stared at Rahab several long minutes before finally translating her words. Pisgah smiled in return, her answer soft and melodious.

"She says that you have that already."

Salmon realized that his sister had noted the looks between Rahab and himself. He colored slightly and Pisgah smiled, one eyebrow lifted.

"I will leave you," she said, rising from her place beside the mat. "I think there is more you wish to say, hmm?"

She chuckled as his face reddened further. He waited until she left before turning back to Rahab.

"First you saved my and Isaachar's lives, now my nephew's. It took great courage to do both."

Her steady look left him discomfited. "The

most amazing thing happened," she told him, wonder evident in her voice. "I didn't realize it at the time, but right before I plunged into the water, I said a prayer to your God. I believe it was He who saved us."

Salmon didn't know what to say. When Rahab started to get up from the mat, he hurried to her side. "What are you about, woman?" he questioned in alarm.

She stared at him in surprise. "I must get home. My family will be worried." She glanced around in indecision. "How long have I been here?"

"It is about two hours until sundown."

Her mouth dropped open. She tried to hurry by him, but he reached out and caught her arm as she swayed dizzily.

"You need to rest. I have already informed your family. Your mother is outside waiting to see you."

She allowed him to help her back to the mat. Their eyes met, and he again sensed that frisson of awareness between them.

"I will send her in." He didn't recognize the hoarse voice as his own. He left the tent, watching as her mother hurried inside. It was some time before he could get his heart rate back to normal.

❧

In the end, it was several days before Rahab's family could leave. Rain had put a stop to any thoughts of travel.

Rahab stood on the hill overlooking the ruins of Jericho. The city no longer burned, but was a scorched reminder of what had been. She didn't hear anyone approach until Salmon spoke behind her.

"Why are you here?" he questioned, his voice laced with irritation.

She wondered why he had searched her out and why he sounded so angry. She shook her head, turning to face him. "I don't know."

Could he sense her pain? Her grief? She somehow doubted it. She still grieved for the people she had betrayed, but above that was this ever-increasing desire to know more about this God of the Israelites. This all-powerful God who could make such city walls fall without any weapons. This God who had lifted her from the raging rivers just when her strength was spent.

"I wish I could know more about your God," she told him softly.

His brown eyes lit with pleasure. "I will be glad to teach you."

She smiled sadly. "There is not time. My family will be leaving on the morrow."

He studied her intently a long moment before he spoke. "You could stay."

Surprised, she narrowed her eyes, wondering at his meaning. She glanced again at the burnt rubble. "I have nowhere to stay."

She watched the muscles twitch in his jaw.

"You could come into my tent."

Anger surged through her at his words. "And what of your laws of purity?" So much for her freedom from a life of having her body used. Her chest heaved with her agitation. "I suppose even you Israelites allow concubines."

"That is true," he told her, unfazed by her anger. "I meant, however, as my wife."

She was so shocked she couldn't speak for several moments. What was he saying? Could he really overlook her previous profession to that extent? How was such a thing possible?

"There is a reason that the Lord has brought us together. I do not think it was by chance that we were directed to your inn."

Could that be true? The thought left her feeling strangely warm inside.

She shook her head and turned back to the city. "And what about my past?"

He took her by the shoulders and turned her to face him. "My people have committed adultery against God time and time again, and yet He always forgives them. Because He loves us," he finished softly.

She met his look and noticed something in his eyes that made her tremble. "But you don't *love* me."

"Perhaps. Perhaps not," he told her honestly. "I know that I am attracted to you. But I also know of your courage, your strength, and your compassion. I also know of your searching heart, and like I told you before, whatever I have is yours. I take my life debts seriously."

Rahab wondered if that would be enough to make a lasting relationship. And what of her family? She already knew that they would never agree to stay with the Israelites.

She looked into Salmon's eyes and realized that he was offering her a chance at a new life. Her family no longer needed her, and she knew with certainty that she would eventually be forced back into prostitution if she stayed among her own people.

She felt something for this man standing before her that she had never allowed herself to feel before. He spoke to that part of her that she had buried away deep inside of herself, the part that yearned for what he had.

Salmon's God cared for him like she knew Salmon would care for her. It was this feeling of belonging that she had missed from her life. Even among her own family whom she loved with all her heart, a part of her had yearned for something more.

Yes, she could so easily love Salmon, if she didn't already.

When he pulled her close and kissed her, her doubts and fears melted away. She opened her eyes and met his dark look. She could see reflected in his eyes his own struggle to understand these feelings surging between them.

"I could have taken you by right of conquest," he told her quietly, "but I wanted you to come willingly."

She didn't answer for several long moments. What would her life be like, living among such people? If they were all like Salmon and his sister, they would be so easy to love. If their God was her God, she would never have to fear again. She smiled.

"I am willing."

He pulled a red cord from inside his tunic, and she stared at him in surprise. It was the cord she had used to hang from her window, the cord that had saved her family's life. He wrapped it around their wrists.

"As this cord binds our bodies, so it binds my life to yours," he told her. He pulled her close with his other arm. "I think I knew it would be so from the moment I set eyes on you."

Rahab lifted her free hand to stroke his bearded chin. Yes, she had known it, too. She repeated her words from before.

"I am willing."

RUTH AND BOAZ
RUTH 1–4

Ruth stared out over the shimmering fields of ripe barley, her brown eyes watering from the intensity of the sunlight. The hot sun burned down upon her tunic-clad figure, reminding her of her parched tongue. She yearned for a cool drink of water, but it was not yet time. She still had a lot of work to do gleaning in the fields.

She pushed a hand against the small of her back, trying to relieve some of the ache. After several hours of bending and stooping, the pain had intensified to a point where she wanted nothing more than to lay down somewhere and stretch out. Thoughts of Naomi waiting for the evening meal spurred her on.

Naomi was more than a mother-in-law to her; she was the mother Ruth had never had. Her own mother wanted nothing to do with her, and especially after she had married Mahlon.

A soft smile curled her lips briefly. Mahlon. He had been her savior, and he hadn't even known it. She had loved him with all her heart, but more so after he had taught her about the God of his people. This God who held life as sacred appealed to her. Her own people of Moab scoffed at such an idea. Ruth was fervently glad she had never had any children, because she couldn't have borne to watch them burn in the fires to Molech.

Pain darkened her soft brown eyes. Mahlon had been killed, and her happy world had come to a quick end. She had fled with Naomi back to this land of her husband's birth, but nothing was the same here. The people despised her. It was only because she was with Naomi that they gave her any courtesy at all.

Someone clearing their throat caused her to turn around, and she found herself confronted by the owner of the field. Though middle-aged, he was a handsome man. His beard and hair were barely tinged with gray. The sinewy strength of him showed clearly that he didn't just oversee the work in his fields, but actually participated in it. At his bold inspection, Ruth cast her look to the ground.

"You are Ruth?" he questioned. "Daughter-in-law of my relative, Naomi?"

Ruth nodded but remained silent.

"My foreman has told me how hard you have worked this day."

She did look at him then. Dark, anxious eyes studied her perspiring face.

"My daughter," he said, surprising Ruth with the title that assured her that she belonged, "listen to me. Don't go and glean in another field and don't go away from here. Stay here with my servant girls."

Surprised, she searched his face, trying to read the meaning behind the words. He pointed to the field beyond.

"Watch the field where the men are harvesting, and follow along after the girls. I have told the men not to touch you. And whenever you are thirsty, go and get a drink from the water jars the men have filled."

That thought alone brought tears to her eyes. Why would this man show such kindness to her when no one else had? She threw herself to the ground, bowing before him.

"Why have I found such favor in your eyes that you notice me—a foreigner?"

He lifted her to her feet, allowing his hands to rest on her forearms. She met his gaze and felt something jump in her heart that she hadn't felt since Mahlon. The feeling was frightening, especially knowing this man's status.

"I have been told all about what you have done for your mother-in-law since the death of your husband—how you left your father and mother and your homeland and came to live with a people you did not know before." His voice deepened with huskiness, and Ruth felt her knees grow weak. "May the Lord repay you for what you have done. May you be richly rewarded by the Lord, the God of Israel, under whose wings you have come to take refuge."

Ruth pulled from his hold, and he dropped his hands with seeming reluctance.

"May I continue to find favor in your eyes, my lord," she said softly. "You have given me comfort and have spoken kindly to your servant—though I do not have the standing of one of your servant girls."

He opened his mouth as though to speak, but no comment was forthcoming. Slowly backing away from her, he turned and hastened away. Ruth watched him go, conflicting feelings warring within her. Biting her lip, she turned back to the work at hand, determined not to encroach on Boaz's kindness.

<hr />

Boaz watched Ruth for the rest of the afternoon. He found her absolutely fascinating. He didn't know how she might be regarded in her own land, but here, she would be considered not very comely, her skin being a great deal too dark. Still, her black hair hung long and straight to her waist, much like the women of his own land. Her eyes were the same shade of brown as his own. It was not so much her looks that fascinated him, but her attitude.

He knew how she had given up everything she knew, and probably loved, and had come with Naomi to a land where she must surely have known she would be despised. She worked harder than any other woman gleaning in the fields around her, yet she never complained or wavered in her dedication.

At mealtime, he was sitting in the shade with other harvesters when he noticed her walking by. She went to the water trough and took a communal cup sitting nearby. Even the way she dipped the cup into the water showed her grace of movement.

"Ruth," he called, capturing her attention, "come over here. Have some bread and dip it in the wine vinegar."

She glanced around at the others nearby, noting their surprised expressions as they stared at Boaz. She hesitated, obviously embarrassed to be the focus of unwanted attention, but finally she made her way to the shelter. When she sat down with the harvesters, Boaz offered her some roasted grain. She ate until she had all she wanted, yet there was still some left over, he had given her so much.

She silently listened as those around her laughed and joked with one another. From time to time, her eyes would lift to his, and Boaz would feel as though he were being drawn into their dark depths. He wondered if she felt the same, especially when soft color stole into her cheeks.

She finally got up to leave without having uttered a word. Boaz watched her leave, reluctant to let her go. If not for the talk that would have ensued, he would have demanded that she stay awhile.

Boaz quietly told the man nearest him, "Even if she gathers among the sheaves, don't embarrass her. Rather, pull out some stalks for her from the bundles and leave them for her to pick up, and don't rebuke her."

The man stared at Boaz, but he knew better than to argue. Nodding his head, he passed the word to the other harvesters. With that, Boaz had to be satisfied.

~— —~

Ruth brought so much grain home with her that Naomi was amazed. The old woman sifted her hands through the kernels.

"Where did you glean today? Where did you work?" she asked in amazement. "Blest be the man who took notice of you!"

Ruth told her about the fields of barley where she had gleaned. "The name of the man I worked with today is Boaz."

Naomi was surprised. Since she had returned, Boaz had done nothing toward helping her, though he was close kin. She studied her daughter-in-law's flushed cheeks and wondered exactly what had transpired between the two.

"The Lord bless him!" Naomi said. "The Lord has not stopped showing His kindness to the living and the dead." Ruth looked puzzled, and

Naomi continued. "That man is our close relative; he is one of our kinsman-redeemers."

Since Ruth had no idea of what she was speaking, Naomi explained it to her as best she could.

Ruth's eyes took on a faraway look, and Naomi's attention was arrested once again. The girl had the look of one smitten.

"He even told me to stay with his workers until they had finished harvesting his grain."

Surprised, Naomi studied the woman more closely. If Ruth were smitten, perhaps the feeling was mutual. Naomi sent up a little prayer while she began to prepare the grain for their supper.

"It will be good for you, my daughter, to go with the girls, because in someone else's field you might be harmed."

The two women exchanged knowing glances. Ruth nodded her head, and Naomi was satisfied.

⁂

Ruth bathed herself, allowing the cool water to trickle over her heated body. What Naomi had suggested to her had her heart pounding in quick-step time. She could feel the warm color not only in her face but all over her body. Could she really bring herself to do it?

After drying off, she took one of her most precious possessions from the chest she had brought with her from Moab. Lifting the stopper from the perfume bottle, she whiffed the fragrance delicately. After dabbing some on her throat, she replaced the stopper in the bottle and returned it to its hiding place.

Naomi helped her put on a clean tunic, all the while chatting as though nothing momentous was about to occur. What if Boaz rejected her? The thought left her cold all over.

"God go with you," Naomi told her, patting her reassuringly on the arm.

Ruth was not reassured. She wandered down to the area where the threshing was being done. The men threw the barley into the air with their great forks, and the wind blew the chaff away. Women sat nearby with basket sieves separating the smaller chaff from the grains of barley and wheat. Ruth could feel their stares as she went by. They were probably wondering what she was doing here since she was not part of the hired workers. She wondered what she was doing here, also. Surely she must be insane to have agreed to this. But, oh, how she wanted it.

After being around Boaz all these weeks, she knew that she was in love with him, but could he love a Moabite woman? He was such a godly man, surely he had someone else in mind for a wife.

When darkness fell, she watched where Boaz went and lay down. It was obvious he was in good spirits. His deep laughter caused her heart to trip even faster.

She waited until he was sound asleep and then did as Naomi had commanded her. Lifting the cover from his feet, she slid under it and lay down.

He shifted slightly and Ruth froze, her heart pounding with dread. What if he should discover her and turn her away? She threw up a little prayer to the Lord asking His blessing on her undertaking. As the darkness deepened, the camp settled into silence, and Ruth found herself finally able to sleep.

❧——❧

Startled into wakefulness, Boaz sat up, trying to recognize the sound that had infiltrated his slumber. He heard nothing save the sound of the crickets singing their song in the dark recesses of the night.

He lowered himself back to his mat and stretched out again. His foot encountered something warm that felt amazingly like a warm body. He sat up even more quickly than he had before, all sleep forgotten. He could just make out the form of a woman lying at his feet.

"Who are you?" he asked hoarsely.

What woman would have the audacity to do such a promiscuous thing? Who would even dare?

"I am your servant Ruth. Spread the corner of your garment over me, since you are a kinsman-redeemer."

Boaz recognized the soft voice, but it took a

moment for the words Ruth had spoken to register. When they did, his eyes widened. *Marriage?* The woman wanted him to marry her?

He moved closer to her until he could make out her features in the dim light of the full moon. His breathing quickened when he thought of her offering herself to him. Of all the men she could have chosen, why would she choose him? Why not one of the younger men who were closer to her in age?

"The Lord bless you, my daughter," he replied softly, his heart pounding against his ribs. "This kindness is greater than that which you showed earlier: You have not run after the younger men, whether rich or poor."

He reached out and took her by the hand, and he felt it trembling within his own larger one. She must surely be terrified, not knowing what he would do. He now realized that his own heart had been inclining toward her ever since he had first met her. Was there any woman like her in all the world?

"And now, my daughter," he reassured her, "don't be afraid. I will do for you all that you ask. All my fellow townsmen know that you are a woman of noble character."

He saw the shine of her eyes through the semidarkness. With his free hand, he gently touched her cheek and felt the wetness there. He suddenly wanted to take her in his arms and hold her close, protect her, and take care of her forever. But then something occurred to him.

"Although it is true that I am near of kin, there is a kinsman-redeemer nearer than I." He could feel her tense, so he rushed on. "Stay here for the night, and in the morning, if he wants to redeem, good; let him redeem."

What was he saying? There was no way he was going to give this woman up. When she tried to remove her hand from his hold, he tightened his grip. "But if he is not willing, I vow that, as surely as the Lord lives, I will do it. Lie here until morning."

He could tell that she wanted to resist, but it would have been folly to try to make it back to town in the darkness. Was she angry? He had said nothing to her of his feelings, but then, how could he? He had to see the elders first. It might not work, but he had a plan.

❧

Ruth's tormented thoughts would not allow her to sleep. This other kinsman-redeemer that Boaz spoke of, who was he? Would she really be handed off to the man like some kind of lamb? No, these Hebrews thought more of their livestock than they did their women!

Her anger simmered just under the surface. She wasn't certain now if she wanted Boaz for a husband or not.

When it was light enough to see, she got up from her place, thinking that Boaz must be asleep. His hand settling around her wrist disabused her of that notion.

"Don't let it be known that a woman came to the threshing floor," he warned her.

Warmth flooded her cheeks at his words. She nodded her head because words suddenly failed her.

"Bring me the shawl you were wearing and hold it out," he commanded softly. When she did so, he poured into it six measures of barley and then put the shawl around her shoulders so that she could hold onto it with one hand while safely clutching the barley with the other hand.

His eyes met hers, and Ruth's mouth went dry. What was it she saw in those dark brown depths? Something that set her blood racing, true, but beyond that she could read an appeal for her trust. The anger she had felt earlier now disappeared.

Nodding her head at his unspoken words, she turned and left him.

❧ ❧

Boaz clutched Dathan's shoe in his hand as the other man walked away. In front of ten elders of the city of Bethlehem, he had relinquished his right to be Ruth's *go'el*, her "protector and redeemer." Boaz was now free to take that job on himself.

Elation swept over him and his face shone

with his joy. Ruth would be his. He was now able to let her know just how much he really thought of her. How much he loved her. He would be her protector from this day forth.

He wasted no time in finding her to tell her so. Still, his heart thrummed with uncertainty. She had asked for his protection, as was her right by law, but did she have any feelings for him whatsoever?

He found her outside grinding the barley he had given her just this morning. She glanced up at his approach, her face turning red with embarrassment. She ducked her face so that he couldn't read her expression. He felt his heart drop. That was not a good sign.

Taking his courage in hand, he approached her. He cleared his throat, and she glanced up at him, her expression veiled.

"I have come to tell you that Dathan has refused to be your go'el."

He saw the quickening of interest in her eyes. Swallowing hard, he tried to force out the words he so wanted to say.

"I will be your protector, Ruth. If you will have me."

Still, she waited. She opened her mouth to speak but remained silent, her luminous eyes boring into his. Boaz could stand it no longer. He had to know.

"Tell me plainly, Ruth. I love you. Do you

think it possible that you could come to love me in time?"

Her face lit with joy, and Boaz's heart pounded so loudly, he thought surely she could hear it.

She dropped the grinding stone to the table. "Oh, Boaz. Is this the truth? You truly love me?"

All he could do was nod. She gazed into his eyes seeking the truth. What she saw must have reassured her, for in the next instant she threw herself into his arms. Quick reflexes on his part kept them from tumbling to the ground.

"Oh, Boaz. I love you, too!"

Boaz pulled back in surprise. He couldn't believe the words he had just heard. Could it be true?

"But I am so much older than you," he objected.

She laughed, tears of joy running down her cheeks. "And I am from that despised Moab."

He met her laughing look, and one corner of his mouth turned up wryly. What was there to say? One didn't turn down a blessing from the Lord. He would take whatever the Lord was good enough to bestow on him.

He kissed her, and her lips spoke to him more clearly than words that she was his and his alone. He had waited on the Lord, and the Lord had been faithful.

JOSEPH AND MARY
Matthew 1; Luke 1–2

Joseph slid the plane over the edge of the table he was preparing. He smiled with satisfaction, rubbing his hands along the smooth edge. This was going to be a piece worthy of a king and would surely bring a good price. Hearing a sound, he glanced up and found Mary, his betrothed, standing in the doorway. Surprised, he laid the tool aside.

"Mary!"

He couldn't help but notice the paleness of her skin and the anxiety that radiated from her large brown eyes. She was frightened of something, and he felt his own protective instincts come to the surface. Ever since they had been children, he had felt the need to care for her, knowing that one day she would be his responsibility. Despite the fact that their parents had promised them to each other years earlier, it had only been a few months ago, after Mary's sixteenth birthday, that the betrothal had been made formal.

Joseph had been in no hurry to rush the situation along. Although he had known Mary all his life, he had never really thought of her in any way other than a child.

Now, he registered for the first time a glow about her. His eyes slid down her figure, and though her tunic covered much, he was surprised to notice that the child had become a woman. Why had he never noticed before that her figure had curved with blossoming womanhood? His pulse began to pound in a rhythm that was heretofore unknown to him and, therefore, very unsettling. He rubbed his fingers nervously over his short, dark beard.

"Joseph, I have something to tell you."

Joseph barely heard the words, so intent was he on this new discovery. He pulled himself from his trancelike state and, brushing the wood shavings aside, motioned her to have a seat on the stool near his woodworking table.

"Is something bothering you?" he asked quietly. He cupped her face gently with his rough palm and lifted her face. "You seem rather pale."

If anything, her paleness increased. Joseph frowned but waited for her to speak. When she did, the words hit him like hammer blows in the stomach. In the matter of a few moments, his world turned into a swirling mass of confusion.

In amongst all her talk of angels and the Messiah, one thing stood out clearly in his mind. Mary was with child, and the child was not his.

As Mary's words came to an end, his eyes darkened with fury.

"And you expect me to believe such a tale?" he rasped. Did she really believe him to be so foolish?

Did she really believe *anyone* would believe such a story?

Lifting her by the forearms from the stool, he shook her slightly, watching as her eyes rounded in fear. His temper, though normally fairly mild, was definitely out of control.

"Who is he?" he demanded through gritted teeth.

She hung limply in his hold, tears running in a silent stream down her cheeks. "I'm telling you the truth! There has been no man."

His fingers tightened, and he wanted to shake her until she confessed the truth. Seeing her wince, he released her. Taking a step backward, he breathed in deeply and brushed an agitated hand through his dark hair. He couldn't bear to look at her.

"Get out of here before I do something I might regret."

"Joseph. . ."

"Go!"

She turned and fled. Joseph slid onto the stool she had so recently vacated. His mind couldn't function clearly. His whole body was shaking. Perhaps he had never really thought of Mary as belonging to him before, but this revelation had certainly changed things. He realized suddenly that he was more possessive than he had supposed.

How could she possibly believe that he would give credence to such a tale? Mary, the mother of the Messiah! After thousands of years, she wanted him to believe that the Messiah was to be born to an unmarried woman. His anger was so great, he was having a hard time controlling his thoughts. If they were not under Roman law, he would have her stoned to death for her adultery! The picture this brought to mind curled his stomach. No, he could never do that. Memories of Mary as a child poured through his mind. Her softness, her innocence. This was too much to take in.

Sighing, he pushed himself away from the table he was working on. There would be no further work today. He had too much to think about.

❦

Joseph blew out the lamp and settled onto his mat. He could hear his parents on the other side of the room, their whispers urgent. He could guess what they were discussing. The same thing that was on his own mind. Mary had left to visit her cousin Elizabeth. He had no doubt that his own attitude had helped to send her on her way.

He was confused. Even knowing that she betrayed him, he found himself wishing it could be otherwise. Somewhere along the line, his childhood love for Mary had changed. The pain of her betrayal went deep, but he couldn't get thoughts of her out of his mind.

He had wrestled with his dilemma for days now,

and the only conclusion he could come to was to quietly divorce Mary. He just couldn't bring himself to take her before the priest and demand the test of purity.

It was some time before his mind would finally shut down and allow sleep to come. Restlessly, he turned on his mat. He dreamed of a man dressed in white who spoke to him, his voice like resounding thunder.

"Joseph, son of David, do not be afraid to take Mary home as your wife, because what is conceived in her is from the Holy Spirit. She will give birth to a son, and you are to give Him the name Jesus, because He will save His people from their sins."

Joseph woke with a start, sweat pouring from his brow. Had it truly been a dream, or had there been an angel of God standing in his room? He looked around him, but all he could hear was his parents' quiet snores from across the room. Taking a deep breath, he tried to quiet his breathing. *Jesus.*

He was to name the child Jesus. He pushed off of his sleeping mat and went to the window. He looked up at the glowing moon in the night sky, knowing there would be no more sleep for him that night.

All of Mary's talk of angels and messages was beginning to work on his own mind. Surely that had to be the answer for the strange dream. Still, the Lord had often spoken to men in dreams in times past. Was it possible? Could he really believe it?

The fact that it had been so hard to imagine Mary in an adulterous situation might have had something to do with it, too. He just couldn't believe it of Mary. In truth, it was far easier to believe in angels than to believe Mary would so dishonor God.

She would be gone for some time. He would think about it further, but he knew which way his mind was leaning. When she returned, he would discuss it with her.

⌒——⌒

Joseph lifted Mary into the cart. Her time was near, but it was necessary for him to go to Bethlehem to register for the census that Caesar Augustus had demanded, and he couldn't bring himself to leave her behind.

He couldn't decide which was worse, taking a decidedly pregnant woman on such a long, arduous trek or leaving her here at the mercy of the townsfolk.

Although he had allowed everyone to believe that the child was his, it hadn't stopped the rumors. It had been hard on Mary. It had been even more so on him. He still hadn't decided in his mind that everything that was happening was of God. Even her own parents doubted her.

Mary met his look and his mouth went dry. The sadness in her eyes was mitigated by the joy he saw lurking behind it. He knew her sadness was due to his withholding himself from her. He seemed powerless to resist her, yet though he often held her close in his arms, his doubts would allow him to go no further. He had yet to make her his wife in the full sense of the word, thus the reason for her sadness. She knew that he didn't quite trust her, no matter how much he wanted to. He had decided to wait until their betrothal period was up and then have the wedding ceremony. It gave both him and Mary breathing space, but taking her into his home before the actual wedding had only made things worse. He would have to do something to rectify the situation.

Even now, the words she had told him weeks ago surfaced in his mind.

"I love you, Joseph. I always have."

He wanted to believe her, but his mind was still having a hard time accepting as fact the story that she had told. He was having a hard time distinguishing dream from reality himself.

He looked up at her sitting so complacently on the seat of the two-wheeled cart. Their eyes met for what seemed an eternity. Regardless of anything that had happened, he loved her. Dragging his gaze away, he went to the head of the cart, and taking the donkey by the reins, he began the long trip to Bethlehem.

❧— —❧

Mary knew that Joseph was struggling with his feelings. Though he was always gentle and tender with her, there was a portion of himself that he held in reserve. She wanted badly to break through that reserve. If not for her understanding of the situation, she might have tried. When Joseph looked at her, she saw the confusion in his eyes.

She sighed, rubbing her swollen abdomen. When they had left Nazareth, she knew that her time was near, but she had refused to be left behind. In truth, she couldn't bear to be parted from Joseph, especially now.

At the pace they had had to keep, it had taken weeks to get to Bethlehem. They should have left earlier, or traveled harder, but ever mindful of her condition, Joseph had refused.

Now they were faced with a dilemma. The town was so crowded with travelers that they had been unable to find a place to stay.

And now she knew with a certainty that the baby was on the way. She flinched again as another contraction took her. Seeing it, Joseph's face paled.

"Wait here. I have an idea."

He disappeared inside an overcrowded inn. Mary sighed. They had already asked this innkeeper for a room, and he had told them there was no room to spare. What did Joseph hope to accomplish here?

He returned a moment later, the look on his face a curious mixture of relief and concern. Taking the donkey by the reins, he began moving their cart toward the end of the street and continued on toward the hills outside the village.

"Where are we going, Joseph?"

"The innkeeper said that we could use his stable. It's just outside of town here in one of the caves."

She heard the hesitation in his voice. Mary shuddered. Her son was to be born in a stable, surrounded by filth. Fortunately, it was spring and the animals would be out in the hill country, so hopefully they would be spared the stench.

She was surprised to find the cave swept out and fairly clean. Joseph arranged a pallet of straw in the corner for her to lie on. Taking a blanket, he threw it over the hay, the whole time muttering to himself.

"What did you say?"

He glared at her. "I said, I *knew* this was a bad idea!"

Mary smiled to herself. It had always been that way with Joseph. Her protector.

"I will be fine," she answered him softly.

"Fine? Mary, you are in labor! I need to go for a midwife."

"There isn't time, Joseph." As another contraction twisted through her, she grabbed his hand, noticing that it was trembling. He bowed his head, his voice shaking.

"Oh, Lord, be merciful!"

When the spasm subsided, Mary placed her fingers under his chin and lifted his face until she could look in his eyes. Her breath came out in short gasps. "He will, Joseph. Remember whose child He is."

Mary sucked in another sharp breath. The time had come.

∽ ‿ ⌒

Joseph watched Mary as she rubbed the babe with the salt she had brought with her. Her face glowed, and he didn't think he had ever seen her more beautiful.

The child lay passive as she bundled the swaddling strips tightly around his body so that his limbs would grow straight. He had to admit, He was a beautiful child. Although a part of him wouldn't allow it, another part of him wanted to take the child as his own. Having seen the babe's entrance into the world, he was filled with wonder. Yes, he had seen sheep and cattle birthed before, but there was something awe inspiring about seeing a human child.

He looked again at the babe. If this child was the Messiah, shouldn't there be something different about Him? He looked like any other child. He felt his doubts begin to rise again.

A sudden commotion at the mouth of the cave brought him spinning around to face the opening. His heart began to hammer in his chest. No doubt brigands roamed these hills and lived among these caves. He hadn't considered that before. He grabbed for his staff and stood prepared to defend his family.

A shepherd came through the opening. Joseph relaxed slightly. Perhaps the man worked for the innkeeper and kept his sheep, and if so, he had every right to be here.

The man looked past Joseph to where Mary lay with the babe. After swaddling the child, she had placed him in the stone manger that was cut into the hillside. Now she placed a protective hand on the babe, her eyes wide with fright.

The shepherd's face grew animated. He turned and yelled through the opening.

"He's here! It's true!"

More shepherds shoved their way into the small cave. They, too, looked past Joseph to the baby.

Joseph knew he was decidedly outnumbered. If these men wished them harm, he would do his best, but he had no doubts who the victor would be.

He stared at the shepherds in surprise when they threw down their staffs and, bowing with their faces to the ground, began to worship his son. Then they told Joseph that angels had come to them while they were out in the fields and told them that they would find the child in Bethlehem and lying in a manger.

"We followed the star," they told Joseph.

"What star?" Joseph questioned, confused.

They stared at him in surprise. "The one outside in the sky above. Have you not seen it?"

In his agitation over Mary's condition, frankly, he hadn't noticed much of anything.

Their joy was unmistakable. "We must tell our families," they told Joseph, still staring in awe at the baby. "We must tell everyone!"

They hurried from the cave, leaving Joseph and Mary alone. Still stunned, Joseph turned back to Mary. He went and knelt by her side.

"Mary." His voice was choked. He owed her such an apology. Her eyes held nothing but love and understanding. "I am so sorry."

She lay her cool fingers over his lips to still his voice. "It's all right, Joseph. I understand."

Joseph looked down at the sleeping child, his whole being filled with reverence. What an awesome responsibility. How was it that the great Lord of heaven had chosen *him* to be the earthly father to His Son? He wasn't worthy. No, he wasn't worthy, but he *would* be. He would raise this child as his own and teach Him the precepts his Father had handed down through the generations.

He looked back at Mary, marveling that God

had chosen her to be the mother of His Son. His Mary. She smiled at him, her love a tangible thing, and he knew that all the barriers that had separated them had been dissolved.

Settling down in the hay beside her, he pulled her close in his arms. How good it felt! How natural. Why had he been such a fool in the first place?

When their eyes met, Joseph's heart almost stopped beating. He kissed her warmly on the lips.

"I love you so much, Mary."

She smiled, her face beatific. "I love you, too, Joseph." Her dark eyes were evocative and inviting, and he wondered if, in her innocence, she had any idea that it was so.

"When can we go home?" she wanted to know.

"Soon," he told her, having no idea of the journey that lay before them. He pulled her closer still. "Soon."

AQUILA AND PRISCILLA
ACTS 18

Priscilla folded the blankets from her bed and placed them in a large woven basket. A lone tear slid down her cheek, and she pushed it away impatiently.

Why should she cry because she and Aquila had to leave Rome? It was a city devoid of God, full of idolatry and promiscuity. There should be no tears at having to leave it, yet now that one had shown itself, others quickly followed in its wake. After all, this had been the only home she had known for most of her life.

Emperor Claudius had expelled all the Jews from Rome. The bickering among Jews and Christian Jews had intensified to a point that the emperor had decided he had had enough. He still didn't see the difference between the two peoples, but one day he would. One day Christianity would rule the world.

Aquila was retrieving their seller's tent from the open-air market. He would have much to do when he returned. The shop next to their living quarters was as yet untouched. She would leave the packing of that to him.

She stopped what she was doing and stared off into the distance. Well could she remember that day so long ago when she had first laid eyes on

Aquila. How strong and handsome he had seemed, especially after having just saved her from being crushed beneath a cart of vegetables. Her eyes grew dreamy with introspection.

∽ ─ ∾

"Ho, get out of the way!"

Priscilla turned to see a cart bearing down upon her. It was dangerous to be on the streets of Rome at night since that was the time horse-drawn vehicles were allowed in the city. Still, her master had sent her on this errand, and she dared not disobey. If she returned without his favorite oil from the pharmacy, she would be beaten for sure.

She turned to get out of the way, but her ankle twisted and she fell to the street instead. The owner of the cart tried to turn it aside, but it was too late. Priscilla closed her eyes, waiting for the inevitable.

Strong hands clamped around her forearms and pulled her to safety just as the cart rolled by. Opening her eyes in surprise, Priscilla saw the Arab merchant glower at her as he passed. He never even bothered to stop.

Glancing over her shoulder, her shocked brown eyes encountered a pair of equally brown ones filled with concern.

"Are you all right?"

The young man helped her to her feet, brushing the dirt from her clothing. Trembling seized her as the events of the past few minutes caught up with her.

"Here, have a seat," he cajoled, leading her to a small stool at the side of a building nearby.

She took a seat thankfully, her legs unable to support her. "Thank you," she breathed, her voice little more than a whisper. "I am all right now."

He knelt before her, his concerned look going from her head to her unshod feet. She in turn briefly studied him. He was a handsome man, and obviously a Jew, since he sported a short, dark beard and a Hebrew coat. She wondered if he, too, was a slave.

When their eyes met again, Priscilla felt her breath catch in her throat. For the first time in her life, she found herself attracted to a man. It was a little disconcerting.

She rose swiftly to her feet, and he followed suit.

"I must go," she said, trying to step around him. When she stepped forward, pain lanced from her foot up her leg. She gave a small cry and would have fallen had the young man not caught her.

His brows furrowed. "You are hurt."

The warmth of his fingers against her arms sent little tingles of awareness along her nerve endings.

"It is just my ankle," she assured him. "I will be fine." But she knew that was not the truth the moment she tried to walk again. He saw her wince.

"No, you are not fine."

Before she knew what was happening, he had lifted her into his arms. Startled, she quickly placed her arms around his neck. He smiled into her surprised eyes.

"Tell me where you need to go."

She would have argued, but she could see by the set of his chin that it would do no good. Since she had no other way of getting home, she acquiesced. She pointed in the direction of the villa.

"My name is Aquila," he told her.

She hesitated but a second. "I am Priscilla."

"Well, Priscilla, what were you doing on the streets of Rome at night? It's a very dangerous place to be."

Horrified, Priscilla couldn't answer. She had failed to reach the pharmacy. Her master would surely be angry, accident or not. He was neither forgiving nor compassionate. Aquila lifted a brow at her and she told him, "My master sent me to get something from the pharmacist."

Something flickered in his eyes. "You are a slave?"

Swallowing hard, she nodded. He said no more until they reached the villa. A servant opened the door and ushered them inside. Her master, Antillus, came from the triclinium, the room used for dining. Seeing Priscilla in Aquila's arms, he frowned.

"Get your hands off my slave!" he commanded.

Aquila set her gently on her feet. "She had an accident and has injured her foot. She cannot walk."

He turned to Priscilla for verification and she nodded, her head down.

One eyebrow lifted superciliously. "I must thank you, then," he told Aquila, though he didn't sound thankful at all.

Nodding, Aquila turned to leave. His eyes met Priscilla's, and she had the feeling that something momentous had just transpired. She watched him go with a sinking heart.

⁓

A noise in the next room brought her back to the present. Aquila had returned. She went to the connecting door, and he glanced up from what he was doing.

"Everything has been taken care of. We have only to pack our things here."

Her Aquila. Her hero. Oh, how she loved him.

He saw the expression on her face and his eyes darkened in response. He came and took her by the shoulders, searching her face. "What is it?"

She wrapped her arms around his waist and leaned her cheek against his chest. As long as she had Aquila, nothing else mattered.

"Nothing," she answered him. "It's just that I love you."

She felt his arms tighten. "And I love you." He pulled back so he could look into her face. His smile brought an answering one from her. He kissed her softly. "Now get out of here and let me finish my work."

❧ ⸺ ❧

Aquila watched Priscilla leave the room and shook his head slightly. *What brought that on?*

He started unpegging the animal hides from the wall and placing them in a large basket. The bone needles, combs, and awls followed. He would leave Priscilla's loom until last. He would need to use some of their savings to purchase a donkey and cart for the journey. He had yet to decide where they would go. He hoped that the Lord would give him a clue.

The Lord. He stopped what he was doing and slid into a chair beside his worktable. How thankful he was to have the Lord in his life. He glanced at the door separating him from his wife. It was because of her that he had found the Messiah. What turbulent times those had been, but nothing like what they were experiencing now. Still, the memories didn't seem so far away.

❧ ⸺ ❧

Aquila glanced up from his work when someone entered his shop. A large man was followed by a small woman. His eyes went wide with recognition. It was the woman he had saved from the vegetable cart. That had been weeks ago, but he had not been able to get her out of his mind. Now, here she was standing in his shop. His prayers to Yahweh on her behalf had been unconscious, yet they had still been fulfilled.

He laid down the comb he used to scrape the furs and went to greet them.

"May I help you?"

He spoke to the man, but his eyes were on Priscilla.

"My master wishes a tent."

His master? He must then be the manager of the estate. "Did he have anything particular in mind?"

"He plans on leaving Rome and returning to Troas. He wants something large and sturdy. Preferably of your best material."

Aquila nodded, his eyes straying once again to Priscilla standing behind the man. He wondered if she even remembered him. When she lifted her eyes to his, he had his answer. The same awareness he had sensed before was still present.

Aquila made arrangements with the manager until they were in agreement. The manager gave him a satisfied smile and then turned to Priscilla.

"Come, Priscilla. Let us finish our shopping in the market."

He left the shop and Priscilla turned to follow.

Aquila placed a restraining hand on her arm. "Wait! I must see you again."

She met his look, hers full of indecision. "I can't."

He couldn't let her go like this. "Please."

She glanced at the door quickly, biting her bottom lip. "If you wish to see me again, you may come in two days to the home of Jason, the fruit vendor on Market Street. Ask him, and he will tell you the way."

Frowning, Aquila opened his mouth to reply, when the manager peeked his head back in the door. He glared at Aquila.

"Come, Priscilla," he commanded, and she hurriedly obeyed him.

Aquila was uncertain what was happening at the home of this Jason, but he was certainly going to find out. His prayers about seeing Priscilla again had been answered, and he wasn't about to let her go now that he had found her. The fact that she was a slave could mean trouble for him, but he didn't care.

❧

It hadn't taken much to find this particular Jason. When Aquila told him that he was a friend of Priscilla, the other man had smiled and welcomed him to his home.

Now, here he sat among dozens of people waiting for Priscilla to arrive. His look went around the room, his forehead furrowed in confusion. What were all these people doing here? Wealthy Romans consorting with poor Jews, how was this possible? Even now he felt as though he were committing some vile sin being in the house of a Gentile, though he hadn't known it at the time.

His thoughts were interrupted when Priscilla entered the room. She noticed him at once and came to sit beside him. All previous thoughts escaped his mind. She was more lovely than he remembered. It was not so much physical beauty, but a cool serenity that soothed his very soul. Her eyes were vividly alive, full of joy. Was that at seeing him again? His thumping heart told him he certainly hoped so.

It finally penetrated into his thinking that this was some kind of meeting. People bowed their heads and began to pray, one after another. Surprised, he glanced at Priscilla and found her head bowed reverently, her eyes closed. *These people are praying to the one true God!*

Knowing that many were Gentiles, Aquila grew affronted. Surely Priscilla knew that associating with Gentiles was forbidden.

He almost decided to leave the meeting, but he had to speak with Priscilla alone, and it was obvious that she had no intention of going anywhere just yet. Surely he wouldn't compromise his beliefs for a woman! He decided to wait until this meeting was over and walk Priscilla home to get to the bottom of this.

Mustering his resolve, he quietly listened to all that was going on around him. These people were discussing the holy scriptures now! Gentiles speaking the words of the prophets! The words they were quoting had to do with prophecies of the coming Messiah.

When they mentioned a man named Jesus, he had his answer. This group was a sect of Nazarenes! A sect that followed after some crucified carpenter, calling themselves Christians. He had heard in the synagogue of these infidels. It sickened him that Priscilla was one of them. But then again, maybe, since she was a woman, she didn't understand the scriptures as she ought. That must be it. He would walk her home and explain things to her. She was involved with something that would cost her her very soul.

Sighing, Aquila brought his thoughts back to the present. In the end, it had been Priscilla who had shown him the fulfillment of the scriptures in the Christ. He was fervently glad that he hadn't been among those calling for his crucifixion, but he knew he was just as much to blame as if he had.

He smiled softly. Priscilla. If not for her. . .it just didn't bear thinking about.

Priscilla smiled fondly at the small amphora of

perfumed oil before she packed it carefully among her personal things. It had been a gift from Aquila before they were married.

How angry he had been to find out that she was a Christian. If not for the very strong attraction they had shared right from the very start, he might not have stayed around long enough to find out the truth. He had been so determined to prove her wrong, but in the end, *he* had come to know the truth.

They had secretly met with the other believers until that fateful day when her master had decided to return to his home. Priscilla had been beside herself because she had no way of getting word to Aquila. She knew that it had not been the Fates that had brought him to the house that day.

⌒ ⌒

"I wish to see your master."

Priscilla recognized the voice although she could not see the man at the door. *Praise God!* He had heard her prayer and answered it. Now she would be able to tell Aquila that she was leaving tomorrow, not in two weeks.

When the servant went to retrieve her master, she quickly made her way to the door. Aquila smiled at her.

"I hoped that I might see you."

She glanced behind her, turning back to him quickly. "I must tell you something quickly. My master is leaving tomorrow instead of in two weeks."

His eyes darkened, his mouth pressing into a tight line. "So that is why he sent instructions to hurry with the tents."

Priscilla heard movement in the hallway and quickly retreated out of sight but still within earshot. She hoped to be able to speak with Aquila again before he left.

She heard Antillus's voice. "So, you have brought the tents I need. Very well, I will retrieve your payment."

"A moment," Aquila replied.

Priscilla moved closer so that she might see what was happening as well as hear.

Antillus looked down his nose at Aquila. "Yes?"

"You have something that I would like to purchase in return."

Priscilla's eyebrows rose in a mirror image of Antillus's.

"Indeed? And what might that be?"

"I would like to purchase your slave Priscilla."

Priscilla's heart began to hammer in her chest. It spoke well of Aquila's feelings for her that he would be willing to part with hard-earned money to purchase her freedom.

Antillus looked dumbfounded. His mouth snapped shut, his eyes sparking angrily. "She is not for sale."

Priscilla knew that if not for the fact that Antillus's wife knew everything going on about her, Priscilla would have long ago been taken to Antillus's bed. Each time he looked at her, she found herself fervently praying for escape. It was only because he feared his wife's wrath that he had left her alone thus far, though his gropings had been many. She shivered, remembering those times.

"I will give you a fair price for her," Aquila told him quietly.

"I said she is not for sale."

Aquila studied him for several seconds. "It was to my understanding that you wished to leave on the morrow."

Antillus frowned. "What has that to do with you?"

Aquila shrugged. "Nothing, except that you may have to travel without your tents."

Gobbling with outrage, Antillus curled his hands into fists. "You can't do that. We made a deal."

Aquila shrugged again. "I will keep to my end of the bargain. Your tents will be ready in two weeks, like we originally agreed."

"I'll take my business elsewhere!"

"You can try, but for what you desire, for a tentmaker to begin now, he will still not be finished for another four weeks."

Priscilla could see that Antillus was cornered. She had overheard him telling his wife that he had to get out of the city right away. She didn't know the particulars, but it had something to do with his business dealings.

Sweat broke out on Antillus's face. He chewed on his bottom lip trying to decide. In the end, his wife decided for him.

Travea came into the room and noticed the visitor at the door. When apprised of the situation, she turned cold eyes on her husband.

"Tell him the price you wish for the girl."

Antillus wouldn't dare argue with his wife. Though he detested her, her father was a powerful Roman senator. He turned angrily to Aquila, demanding a price that made Priscilla's heart stop. Without even blinking, Aquila agreed. Surely he didn't have *that* much money. It was a fortune.

"You will receive your money when I receive mine," he told them.

Travea turned to Antillus. "Give it to him now and let him take the girl."

Gritting his teeth, Antillus called for his treasure box. Opening the lid, he counted out the denarii for the tents and handed it to Aquila.

"That was the agreed-on price. You still owe me thirty denarii."

Priscilla's heart sank. Thirty denarii was a lot of money. What would Aquila do now?

"One moment," Aquila disagreed. "You told me that if I would have the tents ready today, you would double your price. The tents are in a cart outside."

Knowing he was defeated, Antillus counted out the money. Aquila returned half of it to him, smiling.

"Call Priscilla."

❧ ——

How long ago that all seemed now, yet in reality, it had only been a few short years. In that time she had gone from being a slave to being a wife. Aquila had gone from being separated from God by law to being unified to Him by grace. And now they were being forced to leave the only home they had known together, yet she didn't regret it. She would gladly go wherever the Lord led them.

She wondered how her life might have been different if her father hadn't sold her into slavery to repay his debts when she was but a young girl. Well she could remember clutching her palm-frond basket filled with her few belongings.

Yet even that she wouldn't change. If not for that, she would never have met Aquila, for her family was from Palestine. More than likely she would have been raised a good Jewish girl and never have known her Lord.

Praise God that wasn't so!

She felt someone watching her and turned to find Aquila in the doorway. He held his hand out to her and she went to him. He wrapped her in a tight embrace, nuzzling her neck.

"Have I ever told you just how much you mean to me?"

She leaned back, dimpling coquettishly at him. "Have I ever told you that you are a much better master than Antillus?"

His slow smile still had the power to set her heart thrumming wildly in response.

"So, slave," he told her in a wickedly amused voice, "show me just how much you appreciate me."

And Priscilla gladly complied.

Inspirational Library

Beautiful purse/pocket-sized editions of Christian classics bound in flexible leatherette. These books make thoughtful gifts for everyone on your list, including yourself!

When I'm on My Knees   The highly popular collection of devotional thoughts on prayer, especially for women.
  Flexible Leatherette. $4.97

The Bible Promise Book   Over 1,000 promises from God's Word arranged by topic. What does God promise about matters like: Anger, Illness, Jealousy, Love, Money, Old Age, and Mercy? Find out in this book!
  Flexible Leatherette. $3.97

Daily Wisdom for Women   A daily devotional for women seeking biblical wisdom to apply to their lives. Scripture taken from the New American Standard Version of the Bible.
  Flexible Leatherette. $5.97

A Gentle Spirit   With an emphasis on personal spiritual development, this daily devotional for women draws from the best writings of Christian female authors.
  Flexible Leatherette. $5.97

Available wherever books are sold.
Or order from:

Barbour Publishing, Inc.
P.O. Box 719
Uhrichsville, OH 44683
www.barbourbooks.com

If you order by mail, add $2.00 to your order for shipping.
Prices are subject to change without notice.